PRAYERS FOR THE NEW SOCIAL AWAKENING

INSPIRED BY THE NEW SOCIAL CREED

Edited by Christian Iosso
and Elizabeth Hinson-Hasty

Westminster John Knox Press
LOUISVILLE • LONDON

Scripture quotations from the New Revised Standard Version of the Bible are copyright © 1989 by the Division of Christian Education of the National Council of the Churches of Christ in the U.S.A. and are used by permission.

The Social Creed for the Twenty-first Century is a policy statement of the National Council of the Churches of Christ in the USA, adopted by the NCCCUSA General Assembly on November 7, 2007. It was developed by the NCCCUSA's Justice and Advocacy Commission and the Advisory Committee on Social Witness Policy of the Presbyterian Church (U.S.A.). For its part, the NCCCUSA grants permission for use of the Social Creed for this publication.

Book design by Drew Stevens
Cover design by designpointinc.com

First edition
Published by Westminster John Knox Press
Louisville, Kentucky

This book is printed on acid-free paper that meets the American National Standards Institute Z39.48 standard. ∞

PRINTED IN THE UNITED STATES OF AMERICA

08 09 10 11 12 13 14 15 16 17—10 9 8 7 6 5 4 3 2 1

Library of Congress Cataloging-in-Publication Data

Prayers for the new social awakening : inspired by the new social creed / edited by Christian Iosso and Elizabeth Hinson-Hasty. — 1st ed.
    p. cm.
  ISBN 978-0-664-23212-2 (alk. paper)
  1. Prayers. I. Iosso, Christian. II. Hinson-Hasty, Elizabeth L.
  BV245.P8485   2008
  242.8—dc22
                                  2007041810

CONTENTS

PREFACE

"What if we did a book of prayers like Rauschenbusch did?"
The proposal for this book came out of a group praying for a
new social awakening for this twenty-first century. We were
working on a new social creed and the study task force, not
by chance, had within it several owners of Rauschenbusch's
original 1909 volume. Yes, we are historically grounded religious people, Christians still looking for that reign of God,
promised and present, guided by memory and hope.

Although both Presbyterian, we as coeditors—and it was
absolutely a job of equals—stand almost a generation and
region apart. Together on so many crucial matters of faith,
we differ on so many inessentials. But this book is not about
us, or any of the other individual contributors; this book is to
strengthen the faith of particular people and it features particular people sharing their faith at its most personal. It is an
incarnational faith that we share, a communal but not exclusively congregational faith, a faith that sometimes in solitude
wants examples and companions. Some of those companions are here, and we read their prayers with gratitude for
their examples and thanksgiving to the indwelling Spirit in
them. May God read us as we read these prayers.

Part of our collaborative work in soliciting these
prayers was to bring together something of the multi-
colored dreamcoat that is the Christian tradition. Although

fans of Walter Rauschenbusch and Vida Dutton Scudder and other social gospel pioneers, we helped each other discover so many different and wonderful strands in the Christian fabric—a hope of discovery we have for each reader. Not all of those we approached were able or willing to contribute, but it was a valuable experience to hear from many, and to receive their encouragement.

This is an American book; that is, a book of prayers by U.S. citizens, some of immigrant background, as is always right for our country. This reflects the scope of the Social Creeds, but also a discerning for our vocation as church here, in a lurching not-so-super superpower. We need to pray with each other: Orthodox, Quaker, evangelical, mainline, and even those on the edge of faith, testing the spirits, questioning our faith itself. Can the church be awakened and be an awakener to the culture around it— and in it?

We are grateful to so many people who gave us much support in compiling this collection of prayers. Perhaps most important, we are thankful to Bonnie Hoff, administrative assistant for the Advisory Committee on Social Witness Policy, who helped us keep organized as we collected and reviewed nearly 100 prayers. To the members of the Social Creed resolution team: Gloria Albrecht, Patricia Chapman, Gary Dorrien, Nile Harper, Carrie Harris, Ann Rhee Menzie, Dick Poethig, Lidia Serrata-Ledesma, Ron Stone, and Gene TeSelle, thanks for both wise counsel and camaraderie. To our publishers: David Maxwell, Jack Keller, Davis Perkins and other friends at Westminster John Knox, thanks for accepting our assurances that this would become the unique collection that it is. We are struck, now, by the often-long-yeared steadfastness of the saints whose prayers are brought together here. We commend their own prayer books, their vocations and theologies, their struggles, their protests and their lives. Their collective impact on the church's social witness has been profound.

All proceeds from the sales of this book go to support the vision of the Social Creed for the Twenty-first Century through the National Council of Churches of Christ in the U.S.A., and to support Christian social teaching in the Presbyterian Church (U.S.A.) through a journal such as *Church & Society.* Each purchase, then, is a small act of ecumenical solidarity.

Lastly, in this over-hot Louisville summer, we remember a young seminarian on summer internship in this same city many years ago, visiting members and learning about social forces and the industrial captivity of the church in his time. Yes, it was Rauschenbusch. Untamed and uncynical to the last, even when disheartened by events, he had prayed here, too. We hope this book will be read by other beginners in ministry, lay and ordained, as well as by those who have long kept their hands to the gospel plow.

May the social power of Christian faith, which begins wherever "two or three are gathered," be with us all in the great turning and necessary awakening in the years ahead.

Elizabeth Hinson-Hasty
Christian Iosso
Louisville, Kentucky
September 1, 2007

INTRODUCTION

Elizabeth Hinson-Hasty
and Christian Iosso

We are living in a time when Christian people are called to be prophets. The prayers in this book are written to help provide "ears to hear" the voice of God that is calling us and "eyes to see" the reign of God that is spread around us. Our time is a fearful time for many, a time of war and well-advertised fear of terrorism, a time of intensifying global warming, a time of growing economic division within and among most nations affected by globalization. Unprecedented levels of international cooperation are needed to address the problems that we are facing and the divisions among us. People of wisdom and faith are particularly called to speak out and act in hope of realizing God's promises for a new heaven and a *new earth*.

We are also aware that in these times thoughtful Christians are often torn between their concern for crises facing our world and their own thirst for faith-strengthening experiences. Many of us have been working hard and witnessing long for justice and peace, often to see once-clear insights forgotten, good work undone, and needless suffering increased. This book is an effort to provide some of the sustainable spirituality needed for those committed to meeting the social challenges of the twenty-first century. We have gathered almost one hundred prayers written by people of prophetic faith who have been working for social transformation in a variety of ways.

Walter Rauschenbusch's still-innovative *For God and the People: Prayers of the Social Awakening* (1909) has been our inspiration. Rauschenbusch's prayers similarly spoke to a public concerned with the need to change course and a desire to draw deeply from the Christian tradition for guidance in that turning. Like Rauschenbusch, we include prayers related to particular occupations, life situations, and social issues relevant to our time. Unlike him, however, we have chosen to deviate from the basic conception of *For God and the People* as the work of a single author. By virtue of our contributor range, *Prayers for the New Social Awakening* celebrates a richer diversity of experiences, histories, and calls for justice. The contributors include faithful people, primarily Christians but not exclusively so, from many denominations and a range of theological emphases who are scholars, pastors, and activists, as well as several who are most directly affected by social injustice. Many are well known; several have written prayer books of their own; and all have significant experience and wisdom in relation to the specific themes of their prayers.

This book also lifts up another inspiration for concerted action from that earlier Progressive Era: the Social Creed of the Churches of 1908. The 1908 creed was an effective consensus statement of social ideals that helped build support for the social protections of the New Deal and later legislation. Along with the prayers written by a wide range of prophetic Christians we include a copy of a new Social Creed for the Twenty-first Century, designed to build support in our churches for nothing less than the redemptive redirection of United States society. The "social creeds" are part of the social and ecumenical context of these prayers. They call us to be rooted in past struggles for justice and compassion and linked in solidarity with struggles of today and tomorrow.

The Social Gospel as a Spiritual Movement

Around the turn of the twentieth century Christians in the United States worked collaboratively to address the needs of working people and immigrants most affected by the burgeoning industrial machine. These Christians, later called social gospelers, formed a movement pushing both American society and the church toward reforms that would challenge the exploitation of laborers and the tremendous economic disparities between workers and the "captains" of industry. Of course, the theological impulse to world engagement and transformation had been central to Christianity from its beginnings as a Jesus movement. Social gospelers returned to an early Christian emphasis on Jesus' connection with the prophets and teachings about the kingdom. Jesus proclaimed that God's vision for the world stood in sharp contrast to prevailing social practices.

"Blessed are the poor in spirit, for theirs is the kingdom of heaven.
"Blessed are those who mourn, for they will be comforted.
"Blessed are the meek, for they will inherit the earth.
"Blessed are those who hunger and thirst for righteousness, for they will be filled.
"Blessed are the merciful, for they will receive mercy.
"Blessed are the pure in heart, for they will see God.
"Blessed are the peacemakers, for they will be called children of God.
"Blessed are those who are persecuted for righteousness' sake, for theirs is the kingdom of heaven."

—Matt. 5:3–10

These words as they are remembered in Matthew 5 are a key to understanding the social gospelers' ethic—radical and reforming all at once. God's kingdom promised more for those landless then, so it promises more for the homeless or jobless now. Jesus' angle of vision was from below and from a place where righteousness or justice reinforced mercy or charity—but it extended far beyond there. For Walter Rauschenbusch, living into the promise of God's kingdom meant forming new social realities and the eventual "Christianization" of society, despite an equally evident and socially transmitted "kingdom of evil."

Rauschenbusch, the most widely recognized theologian of the social gospel, articulated the theology that fueled the movement in what has become a classic text, *The Theology of the Social Gospel.* His aim was to provide "an adequate intellectual basis for the movement," but that was not his only concern. Rauschenbusch, who had also been a pastor, was concerned that activists and reformers find the sustenance and empowerment they needed to work for social change. In one of her letters to him, Vida Dutton Scudder, an English professor at Wellesley College and a leading voice for the social gospel movement in the Episcopal Church, referred to Rauschenbusch as a "mystic." Scudder and Rauschenbusch agreed that there was a connection between the social and the spiritual. When Rauschenbusch served as a pastor in Hell's Kitchen in New York City, he met with two other pastors and formed what they called a "Society of Jesus." During their meetings they studied the Scriptures and engaged in a variety of spiritual disciplines. We might compare it with a discipleship or support group today, and in their case it lasted for years despite changes in location.

For God and the People: Prayers of the Social Awakening was a collection of Rauschenbusch's prayers uttered in various settings between 1907 and 1909 and then published as a book in 1909. Rauschenbusch intended for the prayer book to serve as a resource that fostered social concern and nurtured the imagination of churches. He focused on the social meaning of prayer in the book's introduction. The Lord's Prayer, he asserted, was the "great charter of all social prayers."[1] The biblical account of Jesus' prayer begins with the word "Our," an expression of Jesus' own "consciousness of human solidarity which was a matter of course in all his thinking."[2] Jesus' words, as Christian communities remembered and continued to pray them, compelled Christians to recognize their oneness with others and to stand together to ask for their common daily bread. But alongside the everydayness of the prayer, Rauschenbusch wanted its revolutionary force understood: the propulsive force of holiness attached to the coming of God's reign on earth. To him, it was a door to the person-making and people-forming power of Jesus, a basic sign of the way personal salvation ushers one into an inherently *social* kingdom of God. In this light, the social gospel movement was a movement of the Spirit, changing the focus of prayer to address massive social evils and seek a yet greater social good.

Prayer and Its Social Impact

Socially conscious prayer today responds to the desire for wholeness that is part of the Spirit's work in every conscience, shaping love and justice to guide both the believer and the church to serve the common good. Prayer is a way of listening for God's voice and finding one's own. Voicing one's concerns through prayer—before God as individuals and in community—raises our own consciousness; enables

1. Walter Rauschenbusch, *For God and the People: Prayers of the Social Awakening* (Boston: Pilgrim Press, 1909), 17.
2. Ibid.

us to hear the voices of those long silenced, even silenced voices in ourselves; and enlivens our imaginations as we listen for God's hopes and dreams. Church membership becomes a form of social solidarity with a resistance to abandoning anyone and an awareness of the dynamic, interdependent relationship between the world and the church.

Every day we are bombarded by stories of people living hardscrabble lives, the horrible effects of war, refugees who will never again find a place to call home, and the unending human exploitation of our natural world. We can easily become overwhelmed and allow ourselves to be silenced and paralyzed in the face of these problems. Vital prayer, however, has an enlivening effect. By listening to God and by sharing in worship and written prayers, we regain a sense of our own interdependence with all things. Prayer breaks the spell of passivity and gives us back our ability to feel for and to connect with God and others; we become more a part of God's loving and transforming work.

For Rauschenbusch, the saving power of the church did not rest "on its institutional character, on its continuity, its ordination, its ministry, or its doctrine."[3] The power of the church rested on the way it nurtured members to be part of what he called a "new apostolate." He and other social gospelers viewed prayer and other forms of worship as a way of reminding the community of faith of its social mission and as a means of turning the church toward its task. In their way of thinking, prayer and social action belonged together.

Quaker spiritual guide Douglas Steere describes prayer as "intimate cooperation with God."[4] To pray puts us at God's disposal and strengthens the rhythm in us between

3. Walter Rauschenbusch, *A Theology for the Social Gospel* (1917; repr. Louisville, KY: WestminsterJohn Knox Press, 1997), 129.

4. Douglas Steere, *Dimensions of Prayer*, with preface by E. Glenn Hinson (1962; repr. Nashville: Upper Room, 1997), 66.

faithful action and a deep contemplation. God thus moves us, we believe, from a concern for our own insufficiencies to a concern for sufficiency in the world, from personal integration to the "need for roots" that we all share. More recently, Latin American liberation theologian Leonardo Boff expressed a similar sentiment when he wrote, "It is not a question of keeping prayer and action in separate compartments, nor of prayer outside of a concrete commitment to the liberation of the oppressed, but rather of prayer inserted in the process of liberation, living out an encounter with God 'in' the encounter with our brothers and sisters."[5] Boff argues for "a unity of prayer-liberation based on a living faith in God existing in all things."[6] Prayer not only finds a place in personal devotion or spaces deemed sacred but also finds voice in and gives rhythm to political action and social practices.

Placing a social emphasis is not meant to instrumentalize prayer or to evade the subtle questions of petitionary prayer and the models of God's action that lie behind all prayer. Prayer in itself is of intrinsic value, connecting us with God's presence and purposes. While the prayers in this book focus on many social issues, we do not draw a line between personal and public prayer concerns. Whatever its focus of attention or resulting benefits, to pray is to respond to the living God, who is both transcendent and immanent. Whenever we pray for others, individually or in large groups, we recognize that it is God who awakens our compassion and takes ego out of our desire.

The public impact of prayer is difficult to assess, yet there are examples of the significant impact prayer has

5. Leonardo Boff, "The Need for Political Saints," *Cross Currents* (Winter 1980–81): 372.

6. Philip Sheldrake, "Christian Spirituality as Way of Living Publicly: A Dialectic of the Mystical and Prophetic," in *Minding the Spirit*, ed. Elizabeth A. Dreyer and Mark S. Burrows (Baltimore: Johns Hopkins University Press, 2005), 288.

made on social movements. The example of warfare averted in South Africa's liberation struggle may pose the question of prayer's social effect in a clear way. How did the end of apartheid come about without the bloody race war that was widely predicted? Divestment and other non-violent international economic pressure from the outside have been shown to have helped the struggle within the country. But it was the nature of that internal struggle that was primary, and it was led, to a large degree, by Christians. A significant moment occurred on June 16, 1985, the day chosen (marking the Soweto killings of June 16, 1976) for "A Call to Prayer for the End of Unjust Rule."

In *When Prayer Makes News*, Allan Boesak, Charles Villa-Vicencio, and other contributors make the case that this call and its "theological rationale" put the actions of the state under God's eye, and the state's legitimacy was found wanting. Churches, ministers, priests, and people were divided by the prophetic nature of this usually priestly act of prayer, and some wondered how one could pray both for a government and for its removal. Boesak argued for the freedom and obedience of the church, based in scriptural passages about obeying God and not human beings, and about finding salvation in no other name than Jesus Christ (Acts 4:10, 12). Villa-Vicencio maintained that true piety included resistance: one's self-offering in prayer led to a continuation of the incarnation in acts of public witness and redemptive action. Other contributors discussed the guidance of World War II–era leaders Karl Barth and Dietrich Bonhoeffer and of Martin Luther King Jr. We may also note that prayers were an integral part of the massive funeral processions and demonstrations that followed the killings of black protesters in apartheid's final years. The impact of prayer remains unquantifiable, but it is hard not to claim that prayer in the churches and in the streets helped end apartheid in a less brutal way than would have otherwise come about.

Social Prayer and the Social Creeds

Prayers for the New Social Awakening emerged from discussions of the Social Creed Resolution Team that the Presbyterian Church (U.S.A.) charged with the task of writing a Social Creed for the Twenty-first Century. The Social Creed for the Twenty-first Century is intended to commemorate the hundredth anniversary of the 1908 "Social Creed" of the Federal Council of Churches, to honor the long history of prophetic witness in which ecumenical churches have been engaged, and to raise awareness among Christians today of the significant attention that needs to be paid to economic, social, and political disparities in the United States and abroad. Creedal statements are often thought of as a way the church defines acceptable individual and communal beliefs. This social creed, however, is not intended to limit conversation; a *social* creed is intended to invite conversation, response, and action.

The Social Creed of 1908 was adopted at the founding meeting of the Federal Council of Churches, a predecessor of what became in 1950 the National Council of Churches of Christ in the U.S.A. Part of the report of the Committee on the Church and Modern Industry, its focus was primarily economic, concerned with working conditions and the abolition of child labor, which is still needed around the world. What is significant is that it advocated social protections not enacted until the New Deal and later, showing a clear prophetic anticipation that was affirmed by the member communions (some of which updated the social creed a number of times). The United Methodist Church must be particularly recognized for its stewardship of the social creed—still part of its *Book of Discipline*—and its current efforts to produce a song version.

In keeping with the ecumenical heritage of the 1908 creed, the Social Creed for the Twenty-first Century also seeks to express a moral consensus among the member communions of the National Council, thus the Presbyterian working group connected with similar groups in the National Council of Churches and the United Methodist Church. Overall, it is a call to a more communitarian Christian social ethic, far more theologically explicit than its predecessors but still retaining some social gospel elements.

As editors of this collection, we, along with the committee that has helped to give the social creed shape, hope that these prayers will draw the church's attention to the concerns it raises. Clearly, we invite members of congregations to pray individually and communally for a new social awakening as represented in that social creed. At the same time, readers of this book may find the contrasts between the 1908 and 2008 social creeds to be an illuminating analogy to the contrasts between Walter Rauschenbusch's prayers and those of our contributors today.

The Gathering of These Prayers and the Use of This Book

The classical movements of prayer are present in this book, though they are not our main organizing principle. Praise, thanksgiving, confession, intercession, even argument with God: many of these prayers move among those elements. Some will fit public occasions and can be read antiphonally; others are poems to be reflected on in silence. The organization of the sections of the book reflects the social setting and focus of the prayers and was influenced by Rauschenbusch. *For God and the People* has sections for prayers of "praise and thanksgiving," prayers "for social groups and classes," "prayers of wrath," and prayers for "the progress of humanity." Our "prayers of protest" approximate his "prayers of wrath"; our "prayers for peace and healing" reflect some concerns in his prayers for "the progress of humanity"; our "communities and institutions" and "various vocations and circumstances" build on his "social groups and classes." We hope our groupings are helpful, but we do not claim ultimacy for them.

It is appropriate that Rauschenbusch's prayer book focused partly on vocation, perhaps the doctrine then most under pressure from the processes of industrialization. Industrialization eliminated much of the individual craft and beauty in work for those laboring in factories. We follow Rauschenbusch with prayers from and for particular vocations, not to sanctify any form of expertise but to share in realms of experience and angles of perception that shed light on our "gifts that differ" and what those diverse gifts offer larger communities. Certainly in each vocation, too, there is the challenge to "sell out," to choose profit over service, to neglect the common good.

Like the early social creed and the social gospel movement itself, scholars have found Rauschenbusch shortsighted with regard to the connections between sexism and racism and society's institutions, structures, and attitudes. Social context, scholars would agree, determines much, and the social gospel movement had conservative elements. Janet F. Fishburn has looked carefully at the Victorian understanding of family and women's roles so prevalent in Rauschenbusch's writing. Others see more support among social gospelers for prohibition of alcohol than more radical positions concerning antilynching protests. Historian Ronald White's *Liberty and Justice for All* challenges this view and reveals a much fuller picture of the social gospel on race, including African American social gospel leaders. W. E. B. DuBois, for example, might now be understood as pursuing a form of social gospel thinking.

In an effort to avoid the social gospelers' shortcomings, we have paid significant attention to the distinctive perspectives added by contributors due to age, gender, race, and ethnicity. More than a hundred contributors over the course of eight months were invited to submit a prayer to this collection. We are pleased to include contributors from the African Methodist Episcopal Church, the Armenian Orthodox Church, Baptist churches (several varieties), the Church of God in Christ, the Christian Church/Disciples of Christ, the Episcopal Church, the Evangelical Lutheran Church in America, the Orthodox Church in America, Metropolitan Community churches, the Presbyterian Church (U.S.A.), the Reformed Church in America, the Roman Catholic Church, the United Church of Christ, the United Methodist Church, and the Society of Friends. We have included prayers from a number of immigrants, but a more worldwide gathering awaits another book.

The editors have not chosen to harmonize the voices of the contributors though one may find a remarkable unity of heart and acknowledged responsibility within the very different voices from across the traditions. The idea of the "kingdom" or reign of God, often in echoes of the Lord's Prayer, still evokes both communal loyalty and world-shaking, in-breaking, transforming power. Yet the idea of God as a "king" is virtually gone among our contributors. God's glory is celebrated, but there is no celebration of a divine authoritarianism. We also did not generally suggest subjects to contributors unless prompted to do so. Rather, to encourage the authenticity and integrity of each individual's prayer, we shared some Rauschenbusch examples and the Social Creed for the Twenty-first Century with each contributor and asked them to voice concerns that grew out of their own work and experience. Readers will also find here prayers written by those who are most affected by economic and social disparities today. We seek not just to pray on behalf of or for but *through* this diversity of voices, to open ourselves to the experiences of others. Thus we learn to pray with them, listening for God's voice in their words as we look toward a new social awakening.

As you read these prayers, please allow them to speak to you. This is not a matter of aesthetic judgment, though we have sought both beauty and clarity. If prayers for the economy have an economy of style, wonderful, but their power is in how they engage us, and some of this power reflects the dedicated lives of their authors. Rauschenbusch's originals, reflecting his own theology, have a parish-inflected tone, Baptist in directness but also liturgical in awareness. Prayers in extremity may not have an obvious inner balance or steady intimacy with God, especially if an evil or loss has upset the world and destroyed loved ones and the capacity to love. Such prayers of lament and search, like Rachel's weeping, may leave us also wandering and wondering and perhaps mourning in empathy. If so, we have heard the implicit call in each prayer, which is partly a call on our own moral compass, our own ability to embody wholeness, our own discomfort with any compromise with corruption.

Concluding Thoughts

To mark a centennial is to reflect on particular gifts from the past, in this case the heritage of the social gospel movement that Rauschenbusch embodied. To mark one centennial is also to hope for another. We hope that those who pray these prayers will not only be moved toward deeper contemplation but also be inspired to act. The church itself, and each individual member of it, carries some of the hope of love's realization in history and is a force for both love and justice. We hope that those who pray these prayers will engage in creative resistance to the powers and principalities that are crushing so many bodies and spirits in our world today.

1

SOCIAL CREEDS OF THE CHURCHES: 1908 AND 2008

The Social Creed of 1908

Federal Council of Churches
(Now, National Council of Churches of Christ in the U.S.A.)

We deem it the duty of all Christian people to concern
themselves directly with certain practical industrial
problems. To us it seems that the Churches must
stand—
For equal rights and complete justice for all men in
all stations of life.
For the right of all men to the opportunity for self-
maintenance, a right ever to be wisely and strongly
safe-guarded against encroachments of every kind.
For the right of workers to some protection against
the hardships often resulting from the swift crisis
of industrial change.
For the principle of conciliation and arbitration in
industrial dissensions.
For the protection of the worker from dangerous
machinery, occupational disease, injuries and
mortality.

For the abolition of child labor.

For such regulation of the conditions of toil for women as shall safeguard the physical and moral health of the community.

For the suppression of the "sweating system."

For the gradual and reasonable reduction of the hours of labor to the lowest practical point, and for that degree of leisure for all which is a condition of the highest human life.

For a release from employment one day in seven.

For a living wage as a minimum in every industry, and for the highest wage that each industry can afford.

For the most equitable division of the products of industry that can ultimately be devised.

For suitable provision for the old age of the workers and for those incapacitated by injury.

For the abatement of poverty.

To the toilers of America and to those who by organized effort are seeking to lift the crushing burdens of the poor, and to reduce the hardships and uphold the dignity of labor, this council sends the greeting of human brotherhood and the pledge of sympathy and of help in a cause which belongs to all who follow Christ

---

A Social Creed
for the Twenty-first Century

We Churches of the United States have a message of hope for a fearful time. Just as the churches responded to the harshness of early Twentieth Century industrialization with a prophetic "Social Creed" in 1908, so in our era of globalization we offer a vision of a society that shares more and consumes less, seeks compassion over suspicion and equality over domination, and finds security in joined hands rather than massed arms. Inspired by Isaiah's vision of a "peaceable kingdom," we honor the dignity of every person and the intrinsic value of every creature, and pray and work for the day when none "labor in vain or bear children for calamity" (Isa. 65:23). We do so as disciples of the One who came "that all may have life, and have it abundantly" (John 10:10), and stand in solidarity with Christians and with all who strive for justice around the globe.

In faith, responding to our Creator, we celebrate the full humanity of each woman, man, and child, all created in the divine image as individuals of infinite worth, by working for:

Full civil, political, and economic rights for women and men of all races.

Abolition of forced labor, human trafficking, and the exploitation of children.

Employment for all, at a family-sustaining living wage, with equal pay for comparable work.

The rights of workers to organize and to share in workplace decisions and productivity growth.

Protection from dangerous working conditions, with time and benefits to enable full family life.

A system of criminal rehabilitation, based on restorative justice and an end to the death penalty.

In the love incarnate in Jesus, despite the world's sufferings and evils, we honor the deep connections within our human family and seek to awaken a new spirit of community, by working for:

Abatement of hunger and poverty and enactment of policies benefiting the most vulnerable.

High quality public education for all and universal, affordable, and accessible healthcare.

An effective program of social security during sickness, disability, and old age.

Tax and budget policies that reduce disparities between rich and poor, strengthen democracy, and provide greater opportunity for everyone within the common good.

Just immigration policies that protect family unity, safeguard workers' rights, require employer accountability, and foster international cooperation.

Sustainable communities marked by affordable housing, access to good jobs, and public safety.

Public service as a high vocation, with real limits on the power of private interests in politics.

In hope sustained by the Holy Spirit, we pledge to be peacemakers in the world and stewards of God's good creation, by working for:

Adoption of simpler lifestyles for those who have enough; grace over greed in economic life.

Access for all to clean air and water and healthy food, through wise care of land and technology.

Sustainable use of earth's resources, promoting alternative energy sources and public transportation with binding covenants to reduce global warming and protect populations most affected.

Equitable global trade and aid that protect local economies, cultures, and livelihoods.

Peacemaking through multilateral diplomacy rather than unilateral force, the abolition of torture, and a strengthening of the United Nations and the rule of international law.

Nuclear disarmament and redirection of military spending to more peaceful and productive uses.

Cooperation and dialogue for peace and environmental justice among the world's religions.

We—individual Christians and churches—commit ourselves to a culture of peace and freedom that embraces non-violence, nurtures character, treasures the environment, and builds community, rooted in a spirituality of inner growth with outward action. We make this commitment together—as members of Christ's body, led by the one Spirit—trusting in the God who makes all things new.

2

PRAYERS OF PRAISE AND THANKSGIVING

Love Divine and Divine Good

Holy and loving God who dwells in light inaccessible, may our days be filled with the mystery of your ever-gracious being, that we may be bearers of a generous, life-giving peace that the world does not give and cannot take away.

For our many blessings, help us to be *appreciative* in the many connotations of the word—perceptive, comprehending, respectful, kindly, discerning, sensitive, enhancing, and above all, grateful.

Make us passionate for justice, refusing to accept or excuse inequality, violence, or oppression. Give us courage especially to banish from the world the evils of white supremacy, male domination, ethnic and sexual exclusion, and all other forms of prejudice.

Make us passionate for peace, cultivating relationships and communities that support the flourishing of life and opposing the vicious cycles of structural and personal violence that ravage the world. Give us courage especially to resist the idolatrous nationalisms that sanctify killing and destruction.

Make us passionate for creation, moved to sustain the beauty and integrity of the natural world. Give us courage especially to relinquish aspects of our way of life that harm the earth entrusted to our care and that deprive others of sharing in its generative bounty.

Eternal Wisdom of Love Divine, give us appreciative hearts in all things and inspire us with your Holy Spirit to serve the Divine Good of justice, peace, and reverence for creation, taking the way of the Word incarnate, Jesus Christ, as our path and life.

Amen.

GARY DORRIEN is Reinhold Niebuhr Professor of Social Ethics at Union Seminary in New York City and professor of religion at Columbia University. An Episcopal priest, he previously served as campus chaplain as well as Parfet Distinguished Professor at Kalamazoo College, while actively participating in a range of social movements. His twelve books include the landmark three-volume history *The Making of American Liberal Theology* (2000, 2002, 2006) and *Imperial Designs: Neoconservatism and the New Pax Americana* (2004).

That We May Know God's Grandeur

O holy One, too often
we resist your rule,
we pass by your glory,
we mistrust your grace.

We divide ourselves between
the privileged and underprivileged,
the acceptable and unacceptable,
us and them.

Too often:

Our religion,
intended to bond us to one another

as well as to you,
becomes another source of division.

Our diversity,
reflecting your many faces,
becomes a cause for concern
rather than gratitude.

Your creation,
revealing your grandeur,
we spoil and devour
rather than respect.

Free us from our closets!
Free us from our tombs!
Free us even from a heaven
    that does not also embrace earth.

Give us, please,
the ecstasy you enjoy
by bringing us together
in friendship, in community, in prayer,
    on earth as in eternity.

Give us, please,
the intimacy you inspire
through mutuality and consensus,
in relationships
    political, sexual, spiritual.

Give us, please,
the compassion you manifest
in your exorbitant love
for creation and all creatures,
    great and small.

Thank you for our opportunities
to make things right,

to make life good,
to be your presence in the world.

We pray this in your many names:
may it be so!

THE REV. CHRIS GLASER is the interim senior pastor of Metropoli-
tan Community Church–San Francisco and a lifelong activist in the
Presbyterian Church (U.S.A.). He is the author of *Uncommon Calling: A
Gay Christian's Struggle to Serve His Church* (1988), *Henri's Mantle: 100
Meditations on Nouwen's Legacy* (2002), and eight other books on prayer,
vocation, and sacramental life.

As We Are Created in Your Likeness

Most Faithful Creator, you have created us in your own
image.

You have given us intelligence to know science so powerful it can destroy your very creations. Is it possible that
you have also given us the wisdom to provide for your
earth and all its treasures?

We can create wonders of beauty and art: is it possible
to still be humbled by the exquisite beauty of your sunrise
or the majesty of your desert sunset?

We have been given the vision to recognize your holy
work: is it possible then to reconsider its destruction?

If you have created us in your image, is it possible to live
without love for all life?

Most Faithful Creator, do not abandon the work of
your hands. Even as we have not loved much, have not
been good stewards, have not glorified your most precious
gift of love, we humbly plead for your mercy and firm
guidance today, at this very moment, that we may know
your presence as we rediscover your likeness within ourselves and all humanity.

Be present to us as we strive to give meaning to the right use of power, as we heal the wounds of war and division, as we clothe our naked brothers and sisters, as we feed the starving, as we quench the thirst for peace with the waters of justice. Bless us with the conviction and passion to sustain us in our work.

As you have created us in your image, grace us with your vision for a whole and healed world for all souls.

Amen.

BISHOP THOMAS J. GUMBLETON was ordained a Roman Catholic priest in 1956. He was named a bishop in 1968. He was among the founders of Pax Christi (U.S.A.) in 1972 and has been a leader in peacemaking ever since, both nationally and internationally. He has responded to countless cries for help in cases of labor exploitation, violence, and social discrimination, showing the instincts of a shepherd when injustice threatens.

For Light and Courage

Benedictus benedicat!
May the blessed One bless us!
Blessed are you, God of all creation.

You created our world with an order awesome and mysterious. The ultimate harmony of the universe, revealed and hidden in your wisdom, both attracts and confuses us. It contains the peaceful rhythms of nature and the violent cycles of life, serene beauty and innocent suffering, the contrasts of flourishing life and desperate poverty, freedom unbound and freedom held in bondage. For a just order in society individuals sacrifice their lives. For the values of your kingdom Jesus was put to death. The mystery of your providence shines in the fragments of joy and gladness that grace our lives but hides within the pervasive hold of injustice and oppression that so marks our human history.

Blessed are you, God of the universe.

We long for a just peace in society and among peoples, but our designs for achieving human community always reflect our own interests, and our efforts fall short. We read your will in Jesus' ministry, but it is hard for us to recognize the effects of your grace in our own actions. The values of your rule shine in the logic of life acted out by Jesus and taught in his words, but we are helpless in following the ways he walked.

Blessed are you, source of wisdom and love, who attend to human life with loving care but whose regard for human society must be tinged with sadness. You have given us intelligence and responsibility, but we see what we have done in the course of our history. We need light and courage.

Gracious God, giver of all good things, we ask enlightenment to know how to apply the ideals of your rule. Illumine the paths that will lead us out of our darkness. You send many prophets who reflect your wisdom. In these later times you have sent Jesus who showed us the way of your truth and goodness. Bless us with deeper vision and more penetrating sight so that we may apply Jesus' wisdom to our societies and find ways out of our frustration.

Gracious God, giver of all good things, we pray for courage to move our heavy limbs. In the power of your Spirit, push us to decisions that will be efficacious. With the impulse of your grace lift up and support our actions that we may sustain them to the end. Turn our desires outside of ourselves, carry them in your love, and bring them decisively to the realization of your kingdom in our world and our communities.

Benedictus benedicat. Come, blessed One, and bless our freedom. Carry it forward so that it may cooperate in your wisdom project in human history. May your will be done on earth.

Amen.

ROGER HAIGHT, S.J., is a visiting professor of Systematic Theology at Union Theological Seminary in New York City. His scholarly work has focused on fundamental issues in doctrinal theology. Haight has recently finished a three-volume work on the church, *Christian Community in History* (Continuum, 2004-2008).

For God's Courage to Witness for Justice and Hope

Creator and Sustainer of the Universe,

We thank you for the courageous witnesses for justice and hope: voices whom we hear crying out from the distant past; voices of the apostles, Augustine, Martin Luther, Henry Highland Garnett, Sojourner Truth, Frederick Douglass, Martin Luther King Jr., Dorothy Day, Fannie Lou Hamer, and countless others neglected in the annals of history. We thank you for establishing your way of justice, peace, community, and truth in the world. We thank you, O God, for revealing yourself as a God who, in Micah's words, requires us to "do justice, love mercy, and walk humbly" with you.

We recognize and celebrate the ways in which you speak to the generations and do the work of justice and liberation through faithful and courageous witness. We thank you for the paradox of faith and suffering; that while suffering refuses to cease, your love, grace, and mercy continue to roar like the gentle Cherokee roses of Georgia. We thank you for the work of liberation and freedom in Jesus Christ, who not only suffers for us but suffers with us in the quest for unity and reconciliation. We thank you for the redemptive sufferings of Jesus Christ that demonstrate your love and solidarity with all of suffering humanity.

In our thanks, we recognize that we have not done what we could do or should do in the quest for justice and liberation. Held hostage by the manufactured desires of Madison Avenue and a culture of profligate consumption, we surrender our desires to you. We are fully aware that you have the ability to establish new disciplines of desires, practices of self-sacrifice, forgiveness, justice, prayer, truth telling, and humility. Our culture celebrates personal autonomy, power, and cognitive reasoning over concern for others and the textured dimensions of life found in art, music, and literature. Yet we hear your persistent call to do better, to live for the other, to seek community and fellowship with you and our brothers and sisters. Liberate us from a gospel concerned only with individual spirituality while disregarding social, economic, and political decay or the systemic realities of poverty, incarceration, and constant preparation for war.

Grace us with your abiding power, love, and mercy to do the work of justice, peace, and reconciliation. Give us grace to speak truth to power; to speak with boldness on behalf of and with the oppressed. Give us grace to find solidarity with those on the margins; those who find themselves living in quiet desperation, ill-health, and isolation. Give us grace to struggle against the evils of racism, sexism, homophobia, ageism, and discrimination against the mentally ill. Give us grace to participate with courage and conviction in God's work as we Christians know it in Jesus Christ, the one who has shown us what it means to heal, to hope, to do justice, to love peace, and to bring reconciliation in the world.

Amen.

JOHNNY HILL, a progressive Baptist, is assistant professor of theology at Louisville Presbyterian Theological Seminary. He is author of *The Theology of Martin Luther King, Jr. and Desmond Mpilo Tutu* (2007) and has an abiding interest in the theology of reconciliation.

To a God Who Defines Justice

"Be compassionate just as your God is compassionate."
—Luke 6:36 alt.

God of Justice,
Your justice feels nothing like ours.
The best we can do is meet some outer measure
while your only measure is you yourself.
Not merely restoring a balance
but tipping everything toward love and communion.

Your justice feels like grace,
like generosity, like love itself.
Your justice is, in fact, mercy and restoration.
It is compassion, filling in all the gaps that we leave
    behind.
Your justice is an almighty and effective love
That leaves no one behind or forgotten,
Not even the so-called unworthy.
We are all worthy simply because you love us.
You restore all things to their original creation
In your heart (Eph. 1:11).

Your justice feels nothing like grudging demand,
obligation, requirement, command,
or prerequisite for love.
It feels like largesse to anyone who knows it.
It forces magnanimity from our stingy souls.
You do not love us because we are just;
You love us so that we can be just
in the same way that you are.

The justified one finally does justice,
just by living and breathing in an utterly new way:
full measure, pressed down, shaken together,
and running over into the world's lap
    (Luke 6:38).

Your perfect justice (supposedly scary)
has never been evident in your dealings with me.
You are not fair to me at all!
When I fail, you only justify me, validate me,
    legitimate my soul
at ever deeper levels,
so I can do the same with others.
No, it does not feel like justice at all.

I guess we understand justice as retribution,
whereas you seek true restoration and re-creation of
    all things
so that all perfection will be found in you,
and through you all things be reconciled in heaven
    and on earth (Col. 1:19–20).
Yet you even allow us to share in your
    perfection.

God of justice,
we are not justified, nor have we done justice,
nor do we enjoy divine justice,
until we share in your own divine generosity.

We offer this prayer because you have first prayed
    it in us,
for us, and with us.
We are only seconding the motion that you made
    first.
Amen.

RICHARD ROHR, a Franciscan priest, founded the Center for Action and Contemplation in New Mexico to unite spiritual wisdom and the passion for justice. Rohr is an internationally recognized author, speaker, and retreat leader whose works show great psychological awareness and commitment to "radical grace."

3

PRAYERS OF PROTEST
AND SOLIDARITY

Against Cheap Labor

Since our mothers and fathers cried out,
since you heard their cries and noticed,
since we left the brick production of Egypt,
since you foiled the production schedules of Pharaoh,
    we have known your name,
    we have sensed your passion,
    we have treasured your vision of justice.

And now we turn to you again,
    you whose precious name we know.
We turn to you because there are
    still impossible production schedules,
    still exploitative systems,
    still cries of pain at injustice,
    still cheap labor that yields misery.

We turn to you in impatience and exasperation,
    wondering,
    "How long?"

Before you answer our pleading question,
    hear our petition.
Since you are not a labor boss and do not set wages,
we bid you, stir up those who can change things:
    in the jaded halls of government;
    in the cynical offices of the corporations;
    amid the voting public too anxious to care;
in the church that thinks too much about purity and
    not enough about wages.

Move, as you moved in ancient Egyptian days;
move the waters and the flocks and the herds
    toward new statutes and regulations,
    new equity and health care,
    new dignity that is not given on the cheap.
We have known now long since
    that you reject *cheap grace*;
we now know as well
    that you reject *cheap labor*.

You God of justice and dignity and equity,
keep the promises you bodied in Jesus,
    that the poor may be first-class members of society;
    that the needy may have good care and respect;
    that the poor earth may rejoice in well-being;
    that we may all come to Sabbath rest together,
        the owner and the worker,
        the leisure class and the labor class,
    all at rest in dignity and justice,
        not on the cheap, but
        in good measure,
        pressed down,
        running over . . . forgiven (Luke 6:37–38).
Amen.

WALTER BRUEGGEMANN is professor emeritus at Columbia Theological Seminary and a minister in the United Church of Christ. A prolific and influential author, his work in the Hebrew Bible has significantly shaped the study of the Bible in both the church and the academy. His most recent books include *Mandate to Difference: An Invitation to the Contemporary Church* (2007) and *The Theology of the Book of Jeremiah* (2007).

⎯⎯⎯⎯ ⟨♋⟩⟨♋⟩ ⎯⎯⎯⎯

For the End of Empire

Most high yet indwelling God,

In Luke 22:25–26, we are told that the kings of this world lord it over others, but it shall not be that way among us. A score of wars and three generations ago, a Christian poet told us that the world would end not with a bang but a whimper.

Behind the bang of war has been the whimper of fear, but it is not the world that is ending, only our imperial view as from on high. The shock and awe of bombs dropped below were indeed awful, but we didn't feel the recoil—though we could see it in friends moving away from us. We were contaminated by the depleted uranium of lost respect.

Jesus warned us to count the cost, as ancient kings calculated the requirements for success in war (Luke 14:28, 31). But we dreamed our financial and military power would always support each other. Was Iraq the war that broke the empire's backing? Or will it be Iran, or Palestine? Or was it the abandonment at home, of the ill-housed, ill-clad, ill-fed, ill-insured, and simply ill? And did some of the church go along with the idea of leaving people—even cities, or lower classes—behind? Could we believe that the suffering of others does not affect us?

God, we pray that in the end we do not amuse ourselves to death, but that we finally wake up. It need not be a great awakening but a real one, to climatic forces now unleashed.

Elegaic is too self-regarding; even lament poems turn away from the blind truth of waste; a culture of narcissism has bred children of wrath. The addicted drown themselves before the force of the wave hits. Dover beach, where the tide of faith was to have gone out, is flooded, and with an undertow of ethno-religious cleansing.

O God, we did for three generations shore up the ruins of modernity, and now our shores are ruined, and more than ours. The anxiety of affluence, the super rich taking without shame, beggaring billions of neighbors, laying off responsibilities, the rhythm of downsizing and outsourcing, the moral silos of high finance . . . even the arts, painted into the same corner as their patrons: may your church stand clear of falling idols. A nation that does not know how to say "when" may not know the hour of its visitation.

Great Lord of nature and history, we know that our days as a superpower are numbered but ask that the landing may somehow be softer than we deserve. No one can deserve such a rich and beautiful country as ours, but for those who trust the flag more than the cross, it will be especially hard.

We cannot ask forgiveness without admitting wrong. There has been too much violence and vanity. For those who blame victims and live to create enemies, the defeat of our delusions will be judgment, not grace. But give your people, we pray, a vision of a right-sized, right-purposed power, so that we offer the right sacrifices, and only to you.

May it be your way among us,

Amen.

CHRISTIAN IOSSO is coordinator of the Advisory Committee on Social Witness Policy of the Presbyterian Church (U.S.A.). Prior to that he served as pastor of the Scarborough (New York) Presbyterian Church and, before that, worked on human rights and corporate responsibility for the United Church of Christ, the United Presbyterian Church, and the National Council of Churches of Christ.

For Persons of Privilege

*For persons privileged by ethnicity, race, gender, sexual prefer-
ence, economic status, class, nationality, age, formal education, occupation, looks, physical or mental abilities, and
whatever else makes us be treated in ways that demean others.*

Dios mío, we pray for all of us who receive privileges crafted
out of oppression and prejudices, privileges that erro-
neously set us apart as superior, better, and more worthy
while marking others as inferior, not as good, even unworthy. Touch our hearts with your motherly love and care so
we will be open to all our sisters and brothers throughout
the world and will be fully respectful of this biosphere in
which we "live, and move, and have our being." Help us to
trust those on whom we depend, who are known to you,
whether we know them or not. Let us see that your justice
goes beyond equality, for though we do not have the same
material, intellectual, and spiritual resources, we share
your equal regard. Change our insistence on claiming we
have the right to use however we wish — or think we merit
or deserve — what we earn. Rather, because the resources
of our world are limited, we must consider the needs of
others before availing ourselves of all that we can buy or
grab. Help us who claim to be fair in our dealings realize
that we never can free ourselves from our own interests
and often act out of our prejudices.

Querido Dios, we pray for the sisters and brothers at
whose expense we enjoy privileges. Give them the strength
to keep hoping and struggling for fullness of life for themselves and their children. Do not allow our injustice to
harden their hearts, embitter them, or have them give up
on those of us who live at their expense.

¡Ay Diosito! Continue to embrace us tenderly. May your love and the struggle of the poor and the oppressed touch our hearts so that we can indeed be part of your family, true children of God, welcomed at the feast of life you have prepared for all those who embrace without exception all of your creation.

Así sea. Amen.

ADA MARÍA ISASI-DÍAZ lived in Cuba until age eighteen, when her family came to the United States and she entered a convent. Her life as a nun included work among the poor of Peru; her concern for women's empowerment led her to leadership in Church Women United; her work as an ethicist at Drew University Theological School has illuminated the lives of Hispanics and others at the margins. Her most recent book is *La Lucha Continues* (2004).

<hr />

To Lament a Nation's Lost Soul

Lord, send us your Word.

Woe! To the number-one nation
that sits unthinking, basking,
in vainglory, no direction!
Almighty Dollar will deny
national collapsing.
Where the patriot's dream? Its cities' gleam
undone by human tears . . .
Its leader's eye
a worried fear
of threats evoked—
who cannot see beyond a *single* year!

Its old citizens, soldiers, and children
languish sick and dying!
Schools crumble, and cities the druglords govern . . .
Her great wealth where?!

While the world grovels for crumbs and drugs,
    Democracy is lying
in the gutter, with filth, sewage, hopes dashed, and
    human sighing.
Genocide and China ply
their trade in Sudan.
Their own leader . . . turns his eye.

O God, you are our hope, and your Son,
rescuer of "lost boys" and refugee "rainbow children."
America! America! Almighty
"God, mend our every flaw.
Confirm our soul in self-control;
our liberty . . . in law."

NANCY C. LEE is associate professor of theology and religion at Elmhurst College in Chicago. Her specialty is the Hebrew Bible with additional work in the intersections of religion and society. She is director and cofounder of the Niebuhr Center at Elmhurst College. Dr. Lee was a Fulbright Fellow in Croatia (and Bosnia) the year after the war ended (1996) and is the author of *The Singers of Lamentations: Cities under Siege, from Ur to Jerusalem to Sarajevo* (Brill, 2002) and the forthcoming *Lyrics of Lament: Injustice, Suffering, Reconciliation* (Fortress), a scriptural, liturgical, cross-cultural, and interfaith study.

To Abolish the Death Penalty

God of compassion,
    You let your rain fall on the just and the unjust. Expand and deepen our hearts so that we may love as you love, even those among us who have caused the greatest pain by taking life. For there is in our land a great cry for vengeance as we fill up death rows and kill the killers in the names of justice, in the name of peace. Jesus, our brother, you suffered execution at the hands of that state, but you did not let hatred overcome you.

Help us to reach out to victims of violence so that our enduring love may help them heal. Holy Spirit of God, you strengthen us in the struggle for justice. Help us to work tirelessly for the abolition of state-sanctioned death and to renew our society in its very heart so that violence will be no more.

Amen.

SISTER HELEN PREJEAN cares for prisoners on death row and works tirelessly for the abolition of the death penalty. Her book *Dead Man Walking* (1994), later made into a popular movie, challenged the practice of capital punishment; *The Death of Innocents* (2005) underlines how many innocent may have been put to death.

━━━━━━━━━━━━━━━━ ⌁ ━━━━━━━━━━━━━━━━

Against Corporate Domination and American Indifference

We cry to you for justice, O Lord, for our soul is weary with the iniquity of greed. Behold our Wall Street magnates, our Gordon Gekkos who bestride the commercial world as if it were their own. It is they who defy you and drain their fellow Americans for gain; it is they who grind down the strength of workers by merciless toil and outsource or downsize them whenever the markets permit such actions. We cry out against them and against the slumlords and developers who manipulate and exploit the poor and make dear the space and air that you have made free; who paralyze the hand of justice by corruption and blind the eyes of the people with lies about welfare queens and illegal immigrants; who nullify by craft the merciful rent-control and minority contractor laws that we by the better angels of our nature have passed in order to protect the weak; who, sometimes in collusion with the church, have gentrified the city against the interests of the poor and have brought upon your church the contempt of the world, all for progress, profit, and ease.

For the oppression of the poor by unrighteous and greedy televangelists who have cloaked their extortion with the gospel of your Christ and name-it-and-claim-it theologies, we cry out for relief and for mercy. We know, O Lord, that you love the weak and poor and hate the grasping and that your doom is upon those who grow rich on the poverty of the people.

Yet we too are afraid, O Lord, because we too seek to be like Donald Trump rather than like Jesus. The thundercloud of your wrath is even now booming over our heads and in our ears, for we share the greed and lust of corporate domination of the poor. In the ruins of dead empires we have read how you have trodden the winepress of your anger when the measure of their sin was full. We know clearly how much we are like them, so we know that the press of your wrath is for us a cup running over. We live as an unjust empire on borrowed time, relying on your undeserved mercy and patience as we pursue life, liberty, and happiness instead of your reign and the year of Jubilee. Lord, we believe. Help our unbelief! Lord, we are sorry, and we repent; but we have put away our sackcloth and ashes in favor of Gucci and bling. Save us from ourselves, from our commitment to mammon, from the indifference we the middle-class have towards the wretched of the earth. Save us from our leaders, whom we have chosen, who have committed us to be the world's police and to chase terrorists with unlimited violence while lusting for foreign oil.

Help us to repent of our ways, to cease and desist from our sins. Help us to turn back to your law lest the mark of the beast, already etched on the right hand of our nation, already drenched in the blood of other nations, becomes a permanent mark of our rebellion against you. Help us to wash that hand by exorcizing our demonic public policy and evil foreign policy, lest our feet be set on the downward path of darkness from which there is no return forever. Lord, we believe. Help our unbelief!

Finally, Lord, in our new-and-improved, internet-driven global village, help us to turn to you with all our hearts and all our souls and all our minds, loving the widow and orphan and sojourner in our land, not as a pastime or hobby, or a charity, but as a royal priesthood, a holy nation, a light upon a hill—a hill that has overturned the tables of the money changers of Wall Street in favor of a genuine solidarity with your blessed poor. We ask, O Lord, that they and the meek inherit your earth. Hear our prayers, O Lord!

Amen.

DARRYL TRIMIEW is the chair of the Department of Philosophy and Religion at Medgar Evers College of the City University of New York. Previously, he was dean of the black church studies program at Crozer/Colgate Rochester Divinity School. Dr. Trimiew is the author of *God Bless the Child That's Got Its Own: The Economic Rights Debate* (1997) and *Voices of the Silenced: The Responsible Self in a Marginalized Community* (1993).

4

PRAYERS FOR PEACE AND HEALING

For an End to Hunger

God of Righteous Bounty,

We are moved by your grace to work for justice for hungry people.

We know that you hear the prayer of the mother in Mozambique whose child is crying for food. We know that you hear the prayer of the father in Minnesota who is trying to make ends meet and feed his family. Be a balm to them, our God, and give them strength as they work to better their lives.

Please hear our prayers as well. We pray that you will give us the conviction to answer your call to serve and to speak out for hungry people.

We pray for the leaders of our nation—the decision makers who can redirect billions of dollars of help and opportunity with the stroke of a pen.

Help them to hear the cries of hungry people that are ringing in our own ears, the cries that are so close to your very heart. Give our leaders the courage, the vision, and the wisdom to help us create a world where all are fed.

Thank you, God, for helping us turn our faith into action, for amplifying our voices. Thank you that when we speak out for hungry people, the miracle of the loaves and fishes happens again and again.

We believe that you are moving in our time to end hunger, and we are grateful that you include us as a part of this great liberation.

We pray in the name of Jesus Christ, who still feeds the multitude.

Amen.

THE REV. DAVID BECKMANN is the president of Bread for the World, a collective Christian voice urging our nation's decision makers to end hunger at home and abroad. Formerly with the World Bank, he is a Lutheran pastor, called at his ordination to serve as a missionary economist.

That We Use Our Voices for Those Long Silenced

Our loving Creator, you teach us that life is sacred. Yet, once again, our country is at war. This time it is in Iraq. Our government leaders tell us we are to put our trust in them and our weapons. We know that never before have we had more powerful weapons. Yet, never before have we felt less secure.

O God, what does this tell us? What are we as people of faith to do? Our shepherds in our churches have become government sheep, and their voices are silent. And each day more and more of our brothers and sisters suffer and die in Iraq.

Loving God, give us wisdom to see that the greatest enemy in our country is ignorance. Help us to realize how little we know about other countries, their cultures, histories, and religious beliefs.

Please God, with this wisdom give us courage so that we may be warriors for peace. Help us to speak clearly and act boldly—always with love in our hearts. Inspire us to be like Bishop Oscar Romero of El Salvador, who used his voice for those whose voices were silenced.

ROY BOURGEOIS served first in the U.S. military before being called to the Roman Catholic priesthood. His increasing concern for torture and murder by military and paramilitary forces, especially in Latin America, brought him to leadership in the movement to close the U.S. military training center for Latin American militaries, long known as the School of the Americas.

⸱⸱⸱⸱⸱

For Jesus' Spirit to Saturate our Lives

God! Help us to become inwardly still—and in that still-ness become so surrendered to your Son Jesus that his spirit saturates our lives. Enable us to know him intimately and to feel his compassion.

We have entered into the joy of his salvation, but now we dare to ask you to allow us to enter into the fellowship of his sufferings. We want you to have our hearts broken by the things that break his heart.

Allow us to be so surrendered to his spirit that we can weep with him as he weeps with African mothers who weep while holding in their hands their malnourished, dying children. We want him to enable us to taste his anguish as he enters into the agonies of Palestinian fathers whose sons and daughters are blown apart by Israeli rock-ets; and of Jewish fathers whose children are torn to pieces by the bombs of Palestinian terrorists. Teach us how to be open to him so that we will respond as he responds to the tortured souls of abused children and to the horrors of bat-tered wives.

God! We believe that if he is in us, even as you are in him, that we will be delivered from complacency when we hear such things as the deaths of thousands of innocents at the hands of soldiers who put loyalty to country above the sacredness of human life.

If he is in us, O God, we know that we will be outraged by that which outrages him, and that it will follow that we will commit ourselves to striving for peace and working for justice on behalf of those who have neither.

We pray that we might share something of his awareness of the evils inherent in political and economic social structures, and that his indwelling presence will give us the courage to stand up for those who are victimized by these principalities and powers.

We especially ask that he be so alive in us that we will be able to understand how we ourselves thoughtlessly contribute to the oppression of poor and weak people.

Then, perhaps, we will have the eyes to see how our cravings for those bargains that sustain our consumer lifestyles necessitate the exploitation of Third World peoples.

Then, perhaps, we will be able to grasp something of our latent racism, sexism, and homophobia.

Then, perhaps, in return for his mercy we will show mercy to others and turn from that retributive justice that demands an eye for an eye and a tooth for a tooth.

What we ask is that he who has begun a good work in us will continue it until that day when all darkness is turned to light, and all sorrows turned to joy. On that day, we know that we shall be what we should be. Until then, by your grace, help us to grow into the fullness of his likeness.

This prayer is in the name of the one whose name is above every name—the name of Jesus.

TONY CAMPOLO, well-known speaker, writer, and leader in evangelical social action, is a Baptist minister and professor emeritus of sociology at Eastern University. Rooted in the Philadelphia area, he has chosen to bridge divisions of race, class, education, and theological perspective in service to Jesus Christ.

For Those Battling Demons

O God, we pray for all those in recovery whose demons
are kept at bay one day at a time;

> for those clean twenty-four hours and wondering if
>   they will make it another day;
> for those in the middle of ninety meetings in ninety
>   days;
> for those whose years clean and sober are like a resur-
>   rection from the dead.

We acknowledge

> all the times they cannot remember and the days of
>   pain they will never be able to forget;
> the families that they lost and the community that they
>   have found;
> the lives they have now that they once could not even
>   have imagined.

We remember those who tried and did not make it. We
pray for all those still out there using today. We pray also
for all of us whose addiction is not heroin but money; not
cocaine but nationalism; not alcohol but ego. May we be
ruthlessly honest with ourselves and willing to admit our
need for you and for others.

O God, when your people wandered in the wilderness,
you nourished them one day at a time. When Jesus and his
friends asked you for what they really needed, it was bread
for today. We confess that there are days when this one-day-
at-a-time business seems like very little, but we are grateful
that there are days when it seems like more than enough.

Let this day be one of those.
Amen.

MIKE CLARK is pastor of St. John's United Methodist Church in Watertown, Massachusetts. He was formerly the Co-Director of the Riverside Church Disarmament Program and Executive Director of Witness for Peace. His current ministry includes significant involvement with folks in recovery.

For America

Lord of nations, we are a nation at war—an endless war against terrorism. We should like to think you are on our side. We are, after all, a democracy. You may have told Israel that the gods of the nations are but idols (Ps. 96:5), but we are sure that does not apply to us. We are a Christian nation, so how could our worship of you be idolatry? Moreover, we are "the greatest nation in human history," which surely means we are uniquely favored by you.

Yet if we are so great, so powerful, so wealthy, why are we a nation that runs on fear? Could it be that our fear is born of our power and wealth? For it seems the more wealth and power we possess, the more vulnerable we become, making us seek more power and wealth. God knows we are tired of this vicious cycle, but we seem to have no alternative but to keep on leading our lives bent on this destruction.

We are hesitant to pray because we are not sure for what we should be praying. We certainly cannot pray for you to rob us of our wealth and power. We could not survive without these things. We often pray that you help us to be just, to care for the poor. But for us justice means that we would prefer to live in a nation in which the poor can become rich and powerful, that is, a nation in which they can be like us.

Lord, have mercy.

At the very least, we ask that you leave us with no illusions, no pretensions, and no presumption of righteousness. Help us remember we are a slave nation that profited by the degradation of your children; a genocidal nation that sought to eliminate the peoples native to this land; a nation built on the exploitation of immigrants and the working poor. Humble us. For only through humiliation do we stand a chance of being honest with ourselves.

So send us some good work to do. May the young—many of whom lead pointless lives of despair—have the habits of their imaginations captured by the world born of your Son's cross and resurrection. May they see the way things are is not the way things have to be. Fill their lives with the lives of Walter Rauschenbusch, Dorothy Day, Gandhi, Martin Luther King Jr., Ella Baker, Will D. Campbell, Wendell Berry—lives of hope. And so enlivened by these who have gone before them, may they (and we) learn to live unafraid.

Amen.

STANLEY HAUERWAS is Gilbert T. Rowe Professor of Theological Ethics at Duke Divinity School. Well-known for his stance on Christian pacifism, he has authored many books that present a contrast model of the church and an ethic of narrative and character formation. He recently published *Matthew: Brazos Theological Commentary on the Bible* (2006) and *The State of the University: Academic Knowledges and the Knowledge of God* (2007).

For Humility in the Use of Biotechnologies

In his *Prayers of the Social Awakening*, Walter Rauschenbusch decried the "materialism and mammonism" of the industrial age. One of his petitions states, "May we leave nothing destroyed by our ambition or deformed by our ignorance, but may we pass along our common heritage more beautiful and more sweet." It is this sentiment that inspires a prayer for humility and care in the use of today's emerging biotechnologies and their application to human life.

Gracious God, author of our creation, we give thanks that in you we are "fearfully and wonderfully" made. We rejoice that in every age you have called men and women to the vocations of science and medicine and by your grace have opened the mysteries of the cosmos to human hearts and minds. In our age we confront the promise and peril of biotechnologies and their potential of altering the human heritage. Such power is too great for us, O Holy One, and we pray for your guidance and grace in the careful and conscientious use of such knowledge.

Hasten to us that we may be disciplined in our stewardship of the human genetic legacy, holding always in appreciative balance wonder and moral obligation. Where science may promote health and alleviate human suffering, guide us in extending its blessings to all your children. Curb our pride and vanity that tempt us to market biotechnologies to the privileged in their quest for greater advantage.

God of justice, through the long ages our sad human saga has provided testimony to our inclination to draw distinctions between races, tribes, clans, and cultures. May our use of biotechnologies not provide a new occasion to deepen such rifts but rather become a source of recognition of our unity drawn from our common image of you. Temper our power to change and alter, and help us do so with humility and deliberation. Counsel us not to be quick to identify "disabilities" in others and ourselves, but rather to see in our destiny brothers and sisters created in your likeness.

Lord of life, provide scientists, marketers, and the whole of our society with a renewed reverence for life. Save us from the degradation of copyrighted life forms and proprietary body parts. Rather, in possession of new knowledge let our highest calling be one of service to the fullest potential for those now living and for generations to come. Let us so craft our laws and customs to reflect our sure belief that biotechnologies stand, like all human knowledge and the whole cosmos, under your sovereignty and the power of your love.

Amen.

THE REV. EILEEN W. LINDNER, PhD, is a Presbyterian pastor who serves as Deputy General Secretary of the National Council of Churches of Christ in the U.S.A. for Research and Planning. She is the editor of the annual *Yearbook of American and Canadian Churches* and several other books, authoring most recently *Thus Far On the Way: Toward a Theology of Child Advocacy* (2006).

To a God Who Cherishes Freedom

O God, who cherishes freedom,
God of freedom and mercy and hope,
we know that you desire all people
to be free.

We remember Joseph,
sold into slavery by his own brothers.

We remember the people of Israel,
forced to labor in the land of Egypt.

We remember the men, women, and children of Africa,
kidnapped and sold, forced from their homeland.
We remember the cruelty of their journey to this country.
We remember the shattering of their families.

But slavery, O God, does not exist only
in the realm of memory.
Today human beings are bought

and sold, trafficked
within and across the boundaries of nations,
including our own.

We know you hear the cries of enslaved people,
we know you see them clearly.
"I know their sufferings," you said to Moses,
"and I have come down to deliver them."

We remember Moses' reluctance to act,
and we struggle against our own reluctance.

For we do not want to think of children
taken from their homes, forced into labor
or war making, or sexual slavery.
We do not want to think of families shattered,
the lives of men and women destroyed.
We do not want to think of the unventilated rooms
where slaves work fourteen, sixteen, eighteen hours a day.
We do not want to think about such things happening
in our country and around the world.

"O my Lord, please send
someone else," Moses begged you.

But you sent Moses.

"O my Lord, please send
someone else," we also beg.

But you are calling us.

You are calling us to remember that every person,
every single person,
is made in your shining image.

You are calling us to remember that bodies
are not commodities
to be bought and sold,
but holy mysteries, reflecting your own glory,
deserving of protection and care.

You are calling us to remember
that if even one member of the human family is enslaved
then none of us is free.

You are calling us to remember
that all creation longs for
the freedom of the glory of the children of God.

You are calling us to remember.
You are calling us to refuse
to turn our eyes away.
You are calling us to see
what you see,
to hear
what you hear.
You are calling us to act.

Amen.

STEPHANIE PAULSELL is a minister in the Christian Church (Disciples of Christ) and Houghton Professor of the Practice of Ministry Studies at Harvard Divinity School. She is the author of *Honoring the Body: Meditations on a Christian Practice* (2002). This prayer of memory and hope is also a protest against slavery.

For Peace

Beloved God, you have shown us through the crucifixion
of Jesus Christ that you feel the pains of the world, the sins

of the world, the griefs of the world. You have shown us that our relentless turn to violence is ever more gall, more nails, more spears. And our hearts cry out in sorrowful confession that we crucify you anew through every pain we inflict upon our world.

Beloved God, you have shown us through the resurrection of Jesus Christ that you receive our ills for the sake of transforming our ills, that you experience our deaths for the sake of renewing our lives, that you feel our many forms of violence for the sake of impelling us to join in your own loving will toward reconciliation and peace.

Beloved God, open us to sharing more deeply your own love for this our world. Pull us into your will toward reconciliation and peace. Transform these agonies of war into agonies for peace, until we yearn for peace so profoundly that we become your channels for its accomplishment.

Through Jesus Christ our crucified and resurrected Lord,

Amen.

MARJORIE HEWITT SUCHOCKI is a United Methodist minister and Ingraham Professor of Theology emerita at Claremont School of Theology. She has been a leading voice for process theology in both the church and the academy. Professor Suchocki served on the Methodist task force that developed a singable version of the Social Creed. Her most recent book is *Divinity and Diversity: A Christian Affirmation of Religious Pluralism* (2003).

For An Extra Push Along the Way

Dear God,

Thank you for this wonderful and beautiful world. It is full of big surprises.

I am trying to do my best in making peace in the world. But I have one question: How can I? Please help me, maybe by giving me an extra push along the way. Sometimes I need a little push but don't know who to ask! If you could help me do anything better, then please tell me.

Thank you.

HARRIET SUDDUTH is nine years old. She attends Chenoweth Elementary School in Louisville, Kentucky. This prayer was written during a Peace Camp held in June 2007 at Covenant Community Church.

For Healing

Great God of all
that is and yet to be,
who knows (ah, mystery!)
what it is to be human.
You know what it is to feel
pain, fear, loneliness, and love.
And you know what it means
to hope. You lived, you live! —
Full in fragility,
whole in brokenness.
with leaden feet, soaring.
odd and outcast, you were,
you are friend.
Wrap me in your life, O God,
and make me yours,
able in so many ways to be.
As I am, take me to be for you
in being for others, too.
Take all I am, and let me be
full in you. I am
right here.

KRISTIN M. SWENSON is assistant professor of religious studies at Virginia Commonwealth University. She is the author of *Living through*

Pain: Psalms and the Search for Wholeness (2005). Swenson's interests include religion and food, ecology, and the ways that people interpret and apply biblical texts.

For Guidance

Lord, please guide my **feet,**
that I may walk in the light of peace.
Guide my **hands,**
that I may stretch them out to those in need.
Guide my **arms,**
that I may embrace your broken children and those
    that I do not know.
Guide my **eyes,**
that I may see the things that unite me with all the
    people of the world.
Guide my **ears,**
that I may hear the weeping of the world.
Guide my **tongue,**
that I may speak only kindness, never destruction.
Guide my **dreams,**
that I may see the hope of the future through the
    despair of the night.
Guide my **thoughts,**
that I may learn how to create a positive change.
Lord, above all, please guide my **heart,**
that I may love all the children of the world, seek
    justice for the oppressed, and live humbly under
    your hope.
In the name of Your grace,

Amen.

AUDREY WHITE is sixteen years old and lives in Dallas, Texas. In 2007, she participated in the Face to Face/Faith to Faith program. Face to Face/Faith to Faith is an international, multifaith youth leadership program of Auburn Theological Seminary in New York City. This year-long program brings together Christian, Jewish, and Muslim teens from the Middle East, Northern Ireland, South Africa, and the United States to develop a new generation of leaders able to negotiate conflict in a multifaith global society.

⬯⬯⬯

To Listen With the Ears of Our Hearts

Forgiving God,
Help us to listen with the ears of our hearts
to the voices of the marginalized
who work for nonviolent social change.

We pray that you will help us to recognize
them as luminous spiritual guides in our midst
who choose nonviolence,
even when their bodies and souls have been tried
by inequity, oppression, and violence.
We ask forgiveness for the times we
have not heard their voices.
May the stories of their faithful lives
break open the hard ground of our hearts,
and nurture in us the seeds of justice and compassion.

Loving God,
Fill us all so completely with your ever-flowing love
that it rolls over the rims of our hearts
and spills into the world in shared acts of peacemaking
with those who have known racism, sexism, poverty,
    and violence.

We pray for your help in
living with kindness,
making love the first motion in all we do,

and in loving one another as brothers and sisters,
because only then will peace follow us wherever we go.

Prophetic God,
Lead us up your holy hill,
hand in hand,
with those who are different from us,
to stand watch together through the long night
of these unraveling times.

We pray for the strength and faith to endure
as we work together
in the social and spiritual gaps of this liminal time,
holding one another's children, sharing songs,
and offering beams of hope,
by letting our collective lives reflect,
in the rising sun of this great turning,
what the power of Love can do.
Amen.

CATHY WHITMIRE is a retreat leader, author, and anthologist within
the Society of Friends. She recently published *Practicing Peace* (2007),
which shares her tradition's 350-year-old practice of peaceable living
with spiritual seekers of all religions.

For Peace

Jesus had a very specific understanding about prayer, which
he teaches us in Mark 11:22–24: "'Have faith in God. Truly
I tell you, if you say to this mountain, "Be taken up and
thrown into the sea," and if you do not doubt in your heart,
but believe that what you say will come to pass, it will be
done for you. So I tell you, whatever you ask for in prayer,
believe that you have received it, and it will be yours.'" He
does not utter a prayer and then await its coming about some

time in the future. Rather, he tells us to visualize it as already in the process of happening: "'Believe that what you say will come to pass.'" The Greek is even more emphatic: "'It is happening [*ho lalei ginetai*],'" now, despite all appearances. We must see God's response as already taking place. Faith, then, is living in the completion of our prayer.

Greg Brandon, at the Science and Consciousness Convention in Santa Fe in 2006, tells of a Native American friend named David who invited him to walk over to a sacred medicine wheel to pray for rain. It was the worst drought in New Mexico history. The Rio Grande was dry. When they arrived, David took off his shoes and put his feet in the circle, announcing, "All of my ancestors are with me now, are with me now." Then he looked at his watch and declared, "Let's eat."

Greg thought that at the very least they should first offer their prayers.

"No. I didn't come here to pray for rain. Because if I prayed for rain, rain could never happen. Because the moment you pray for something you are acknowledging that it doesn't exist in the moment. If our consciousness is having an effect on things, and we are saying, 'Please, let there be rain, dear God, please bring rain,' we are perpetuating drought. If we ask for peace, or healing, we mean well, but are we really helping?"

Greg asks, "Weren't you praying for rain when your eyes were closed?"

David replied, "When I closed my eyes, I was experiencing the feeling of mud between my toes, because there's so much mud, because there's been so much rain. I smelled the smell of the adobe houses when they are wet, and felt what it feels like to run with my shirt off through the standing corn that is so high because there's been so much rain. And I gave thanks for the rain that has already fallen."

Big black clouds formed. By the third day there was flooding.

Greg: "How do you stop this rain?"

David: "I don't know!"

Will you join me in a bidding prayer that invites us to visualize a world being transformed? Pick a place that excites your compassion, and hold it in your inner vision for at least five minutes, or however long it takes to bring it into focus. What you say will come to pass. It is happening, it is happening. Thank God for bringing your prayer to pass.

WALTER WINK is a biblical scholar and JUNE KEENER WINK is a potter. The Winks have led workshops across the church and internationally. Walter, a pioneer in transforming Bible study, is now best known for his groundbreaking trilogy on "The Powers." Walter and June together use psychological and experiential approaches to disarm structures of domination and nurture communities of hope.

<hr>

A Prayer for Summer Sabbath Reflection

I

O Thou who hast declared that the lion and the lamb shall lie down together, that we are to be led by trust as innocent and straightforward as that of a little child, empty us of angry judgments and aching disappointments. As we consider the blessings of our lives (family ties and summer reunions, worship in and service through thy church, the stewardship of money and time and talent) give us, most of all, grateful hearts.

Breathe into us, O God, quietness and confidence. Catch our doubts and pride off guard, so that we may sense thy presence and thy gracious caring. Surprise us with joy.

II

The heat of summer bears down on us, O God, and we pray for those who suffer because of their age or their poverty or their class. Recent days have taught us again about the widening gap between those who have more than most can imagine and those who have so little.

We pray especially for those who do not have, but we ask thee also to spur generosity in those of us who have much. Awaken new compassion within us for the poor, the children, the aging, the sick, and the fearful. Grant all of them peace, sustenance, hope, and abundant life.

III

Dear God, we pray for ourselves in a minor key. We want a place where we can belong, so teach us to accept each other. We want to have close friends, so teach us to reach out. We want mercy, so teach us to forgive. We want beauty, so we ask for honesty. We want peace, so lead us to the eye of the storm. We want truth, so teach us to question our unquestionable convictions. We desire joy, so show us the way to deeper commitment.

O persistent and loving and gracious God, deliver us from assuming that thy mercy is always gentle. If we are too self-satisfied, put pressure on us about our lack of humility. If we worry about all the problems that plague thy world, deepen the hurt within us enough to make us want to serve the least, the last, and the lost. If we are afraid to look at our prejudices, accentuate our confusion enough to make us change our minds. Pry us out of our spiritual holes and put us on the right path again; through Jesus Christ our Lord.

JAMES WINKLER is the general secretary of the General Board of Church and Society of the United Methodist Church, Washington, DC. A layperson, he coordinates the social witness of the United Methodist Church not only in the Capitol, but through education and spiritual life resources throughout the denomination.

5

PRAYERS
FOR COMMUNITIES
AND INSTITUTIONS

As We Discern Our Vocation

Lord, make us mindful of our vocation
that we make no excuses in the face of injustice and
    oppression,
that we see the suffering of those who are crucified
    today,
so that you don't condemn us.
For if we have not done for the least, we have not done
    for you.

Remind us, O Lord, that even in our worst prisons,
our voices are indeed free to speak out against oppres-
    sion and tyranny;
our souls are free to envision and proclaim the day that
    has been promised;
the day when the hard mountains of oppression will
    blow away like wisps of cotton;
when this earth will quake and lightning flash angrily
    over the heads of oppressors and despots;

when all the crowns will be tossed in the air and the
    thrones will be destroyed and sovereignty will
    belong to the people;
when the mighty are brought down and the lowly
    raised, prisoners set free, the hungry fed, the naked
    clothed, the blind see, the untouchables embraced;
when the lion will lie down with the lamb.

God of justice and peace, make us your instruments so
    that we struggle to ensure
that there is no wealth without work;
no pleasure without conscience;
no technology and science without humanity and care
    for your creation;
no knowledge without character and compassion;
no politics without principle;
no commerce without morality and ethics;
and no worship without sacrifice.

We pray in the name of the one who truly worshiped
    through sacrifice,
our Pascal Lamb Jesus Christ.
Amen.

CHARLES AMJAD-ALI is the Martin Luther King Jr. Professor of Justice and Christian Community and also the director of the Islamic Studies
Program at Luther Seminary in St. Paul, Minnesota. Formerly director of
the Christian Institute in Pakistan, he has been active in national and
international civil society institutions and has published extensively. This
prayer adapts Gandhi's seven social sins in its final section.

⌒⌒⌒⌒

For the Church

Most merciful God, help us in our time of fragmentation and
isolation, when our society tells us we are alone and can rely

only on ourselves. Remind us again of the truth you sent to us through your son, Jesus Christ, that we are one with him as he is one with you, that in the church we are part of the body of Christ and our salvation comes only through our membership in that body. Our society tells us to estimate the return from every relationship, even the most intimate, and to ignore those ties that are not sufficiently profitable. It tells us that working to alleviate poverty and injustice will not help us get ahead. Remind us how far those teachings are from yours. Remind us that only in losing ourselves will we find ourselves, that we are one with every human being, and that we will not be free until all are free. Your son is offered up for us in every Communion service that through him and with others we will be saved. Remind us, as we struggle against the currents of our day, that our joy is not in our possessions but in offering up ourselves as communion for others. Help us to hear the whole creation crying out for reunion and to realize that we will find salvation only in responding to that cry, through Jesus Christ our Lord.

Amen.

ROBERT BELLAH is a seminal thinker in sociology and religious studies. Best known as lead author of *Habits of the Heart* and its successor, *The Good Society*, Bellah has developed insights on civil religion, religious evolution and pluralism, American culture and community that have been significant in several disciplines and in public policy. *The Robert Bellah Reader* (2006) brings together major essays, key articles, and even three sermons.

For High-Quality Education for All

God, the Creator and Sustainer, we pray for continuing opportunities to cultivate our minds at every stage of life. We no longer want to mute sounds struggling to speak nor deny creative questions that expand our horizon. Teach us to appreciate the uncommonly common folks who face adversity after adversity, especially women, men, and children relegated to back-breaking labor, who nonetheless hunger to acquire knowledge and skills.

We thank you for mercifully granting us healing from pain-filled yesteryears and difficult bygone days, when wailing tears rattled in our throats and legitimate dreams of going to public libraries and participating in spelling contests were lassoed by lies of law and order, justifying reality as separate but yet unequal. We pray that no more lies hinder children not unlike our own; no more boundaries contain them from within.

Disarm us with artistic delight, cheerful melodies, and the awe of mystery as we celebrate joyful learning. Give us this day new sites of inquiry, courage to explore, and opportunities to experiment. Keep us safe as we go hither and thither, staying open-minded, ready to entertain fresh ideas about what counts as wisdom. Renew in us wonder for the sanctity of the named and unnamed. And even when we are startled by unbelievable paradoxes, reawaken in us energizing modes of giving and receiving so that usable truth can emerge.

Grant us grace, O God, to appreciate the numerous ways in which you continue to turn around disappointments with unsuspecting gifts. Help us remember those throughout the world whose hand-me-down stories serve as counternarratives to texts full of definitions and directions developed elsewhere. Like boisterous thunderstorms and silent whispers, allow our words to act in the name of justice.

Amen.

KATIE GENEVA CANNON is the Annie Scales Rogers Professor of Christian Ethics at Union-PSCE in Richmond, Virginia. The first African American woman ordained in the United Presbyterian Church (U.S.A.), she has been a leader in the field of Christian ethics, womanist theology, and women in religion and society. She has lectured nationally on theological and ethical topics and is the author or editor of numerous articles and seven books including *Katie's Canon: Womanism and the Soul of the Black Community* (1997) and *Black Womanist Ethics* (1988).

<hr />

To Embody a God of Hope and Healing

Dear God, you are the Creator and Sustainer of all that is, the ineffable One, the Beyond and the Now. In the presence of your imponderable reality, your love, and your truth, give us the capacity to be empty, humble, and relaxed. Seep into our depths. Help us to sink more deeply into yours. You long for us to embody you, to become a unique corporate expression of your fullest being. Search us and know us, root out whatever keeps us from letting you make your home in us, and draw us deeper into the waters of your mercy and love.

God of hope and healing, we bring to you not only our own wandering and beleaguered selves, but all who live in misery and loss. We bring the children who are trapped in poverty, and especially the 32,000 who today and tomorrow and the day after will die of treatable causes. We bring their parents, who feel desperately helpless and alone. We bring the world's prisoners, who long for someone to listen and care, and for the opportunity of reconciliation. We bring those searching endlessly for meaningful work adequate to meet their families' needs. We bring our sisters and brothers all around the world who are fleeing from one place of strife to another. We bring our entire family, yearning to be healed, to be freed. We sink now into the awareness that we are one people, one body, made in your likeness and your love.

We know you are a God of miracles, and we offer ourselves to be used as a channel of your miracle-making power. Draw us into your healing, freeing flow so that corporately we might become the stream of love you and our groaning world long for us to be. Carry us where we have been reluctant to go, into the undiscovered dimensions of ourselves and our human family, which we have resisted entering fully. May the resurrected and resurrecting love of Jesus Christ pour into us and, through us, into the world. Together with him, we long to be more fully in you and in one another. For the sake of your realm among us becoming reality, on earth as it is in heaven, we pray.

Amen.

GORDON COSBY along with his wife, Mary, founded The Church of the Saviour in Washington, DC, in 1947. Now several small churches, The Church of the Saviour has helped Christians from all over the United States to identify their own sense of call. A network of ministries designed to address the needs of poor people living in the sprawling DC urban area continues to be inspired and supported by The Church of the Saviour.

For Strength to Fight for Justice

O Lord my God, have mercy upon me when I feel lost and discouraged by the prevalent evils of these days. Like the psalmist, I too dwell in the shadow of the valley of death. This is a world that has traded the worship of the Creator for seeking the pleasuring of modern gods. We approach the altar of commerce to bow our knees to the false gods of money and profit. Like Molech of old, the god of capital is appeased through the daily sacrifice of thirty thousand children who die of hunger and preventable diseases. I confess, dear God, that I have lost my hope as I witness the carnage caused by the globalization of the economy. The few get richer as the many sink to greater depths of poverty and marginalization.

Could it be that *El Roi*, the God who sees, is blind to the miseries faced by the world's dispossessed? Is *Jehovah-jireh*, the God who will provide, impotent to giving the disenfranchised their daily bread? How can *Jehovah-rophe*, the God who heals, be unable to cure what ails the world's marginalized?

O Lord, why do you delay bringing about the justice and righteousness that, as Amos reminds us, should roll down like water and flow like an unfailing stream? I confess my anger toward the global social structures designed to provide the minority with obscene amounts of power and privilege. If you did not hold the answers to truth and life, I would have abandoned your ways long ago. So I come to you, *Jehovah-shalom*, the God of peace, praying that you restore in me a new spirit. A spirit that can see with eternal eyes, so that in the darkness of the hour I do not forget the truths that were so clear in the brightness of your presence.

Strengthen me to continue fighting valiantly for justice by standing faithfully with the hungry, the thirsty, the naked, the alien, the imprisoned, and the sick. In the hopelessness of our postmodern times, show me how to hope against all hope. Teach me that my calling to bring about your salvation and liberation is not limited to the span of my lifetime. Though it might not be my eyes, nor the eyes of my children, nor their children's children, that witness the fulfillment of your glory, I commit to remain in solidarity with the least of these, reassured that the seeds planted in the night may one day—long after this mortal body is consumed by worms—bear fruit in the light of day. Let my final reward be to hear your voice saying, "Well done, my good and faithful servant."

Amen.

MIGUEL A. DE LA TORRE is the director of Iliff School of Theology's Justice and Peace Institute and serves as associate professor for social ethics. The focus of his academic pursuit has been social and political ethics within contemporary U.S. thought, specifically how religion affects race, class, and gender oppression. He has contributed to and authored many books, including *Doing Christian Ethics from the Margins* (2004).

For the Church as We Proclaim the Gospel

Guard your church, O God,
from illusions of grandeur,
from obeisance to power,
from vanity that demands notice.

Guard your church, O God,
from certainty that exterminates novelty,
from uncertainty that precludes action,
from neutrality that blesses what is.

Guard your church, O God,
from arrogance that speaks for others,
from dalliance that trivializes agony,
from advocacy that tinkers at transformation.

Guard your church, O God,
from cowardice during times of contention,
from capitulation to threats without and within,
from charity that perpetuates inequality.

Guard your church, O God,
from pity that precludes partnership,
from heroics that disintegrate democracy,
from procedure that prolongs injustice.

Guard your church, O God.
Awaken us in mercy,
strengthen us in crucifixion,
forge us in resurrection,
that we may give
though it make us insecure;
that we may depend
though it offend our pride;

that we may challenge
though it cost our reputation;
that we may hope
though it seems unreasonable;
that we may love
though scorn feels righteous;
that we may build
though tearing down be expedient;
that we may speak
though silence would be safer;
that we may venture
though we may not see the end.

Guard your church, O God.
In the strong name of Jesus Christ we pray.
Amen.

THE REV. NOELLE DAMICO coordinates the Presbyterian Church
(U.S.A.)'s Campaign for Fair Food, an effort to establish human rights
for farm workers and socially responsible purchasing within the retail-
food industry (www.pcusa.org/fairfood). She has collaborated with
poor people's organizations to convince major corporations and government officials to use their power to improve wages and working
conditions for laborers at the base of their supply chains, particularly
day laborers harvesting tomatoes in Florida and labor pool workers
cleaning Camden Yards stadium in Baltimore. An ordained minister in
the United Church of Christ, she also serves as catalyst for the University of the Poor, School of Theology (www.universityofthepoor.org).
Her published work includes songs, liturgy, and biblical and theological commentary that place justice-seeking at the heart of faith.

That We May Be Satisfied

Generous God,
Enough is enough! Or is it? Your love and care are
extended to us way beyond our deserving, way beyond our

capacity to collect. You provide us more than enough. Indeed, in pulpit and in heart we proclaim, "God's grace is sufficient. God's grace is enough."

But Lord, so much of life disclaims that enoughness.

We hope for more than we need.

We work for more than we can obtain.

We demand more than we have earned.

We expect more than our share.

At the same time we hear story upon story of people truly lacking the enough we consider so basic to our lives. Refugees, migrants, and the homeless may have a place, but they inhabit only a nowhere and only for the moment. They may even have a spot to rest their heads, but a folded newspaper or pile of twigs hardly qualifies as a pillow the rest of us would choose.

Too many millions of children lack the basic nutrients with which to build strong bodies, as famine and adult power struggles strip their pantries bare. And, let's face it, God. One hungry child would be too many for the rest of us to abide.

In pockets of conflict around the world, too many can't even catch a quiet night's sleep, as gunshots and bombs explode their peace.

God, we *do* affirm your enoughness. Please, now, bestow on those so lacking: the home, the food, and the peace they need truly to have enough. And help us who enjoy a super-abundance to turn our longing for more into a mission to simplify, to share, and to follow your lead, that is, to give.

In the name of the one who gave himself, even Christ Jesus our Lord, we pray.

Amen.

JACK HABERER is editor of the independent journal *The Presbyterian Outlook* and author of *Godviews* (2001), an analysis of major faith tendencies found in mainline Protestantism. He has served as a pastor and leader in evangelical Presbyterianism.

To See Tax and Budget Policy
as a Vehicle of God's Justice

Dear God,

Provide us the spiritual wisdom to see tax and budget policy as an important vehicle to carry out your standards of justice.

Remind us that your standards of justice require that all of us, especially the poor, weak, and vulnerable, have a reasonable opportunity to develop the divinely inspired potential you created in your image in each of us.

Remind us that your standards of justice cross all boundaries of time and culture, and that for our time and culture reasonable opportunity means each person must have access to adequate education, healthcare, housing, subsistence, and a fair and living wage.

Remind us that our inescapable tendency to succumb to the sin of greed means you cannot count on us to contribute voluntarily our fair share needed to meet your standards of justice.

For that reason, help us accept the yoke of compulsory taxation as a vital part of your plan for achieving justice and resisting selfishness.

Remind us that in addition to raising adequate revenues to support reasonable opportunity for all, the standards of justice embodied in your teachings on wealth and the moral obligation "to whom much is given, much more is required" mean that those of us enjoying greater levels of wealth must proportionally bear a greater share of the tax burden. Save us from rejecting your ethical claim, in hopes that enthusiastic worship, passionate concern over issues that cost us little, and charitable giving alone could render us truly faithful.

Save us from rejecting your message, by the ungrateful claim that our wealth comes solely from our own efforts.

Remind us that by your grace and mercy you give us the ability to produce wealth and you are the sole source of wealth.

Remind us that those blessed with a greater share of your wealth must show a higher level of sacrificial discipleship as stewards for your kingdom on Earth, which includes supporting tax and budget policies that meet your standards of justice.

O Lord,

Give those of us blessed with greater shares of your wealth the passion and energy we need to spread your message of faith-inspired tax policy across America and the world, for it is difficult to support laws imposing greater sacrifices on us.

Give those of us with little wealth the courage we need to embrace your message of faith-inspired tax policy and make the best of the reasonable opportunity available to us, for it is always difficult to support the unknown in the midst of lies and distortions intended to mislead us.

Give all of us willing to stand for your message of faith-inspired tax policy the strength we need to face the fierce opposition we will encounter, for the forces of evil feeding on the sin of greed are working overtime to kill your message.

I make this prayer in the name of your son, our Lord and Savior Jesus Christ.

Amen.

SUSAN PACE HAMILL, a United Methodist, has attracted enormous attention for her ethical critiques of Alabama's tax code and President George W. Bush's first-term tax cuts. After practicing tax law in a "white shoe" New York firm and for the IRS, she now teaches at the University of Alabama's Law School. Her application of biblical moral principles to tax policy continues in her most recent book, *As Certain as Death: A Fifty-State Survey of State and Local Tax Laws* (2007).

For Ecumenical Witness

God our Creator, we pray for your church, sign of your reconciling love in a world of fearful division, instrument of your compassionate justice in a world of frequent oppression. We give thanks for those times when the church has nurtured us in the ways of peace and for those leaders of the church who have challenged the society of their day to address the needs of the poor. But we also lament those times when we, the church, have been lukewarm in the cause of justice and when we have settled for comfortable separation rather than daring to receive your gift of unity in Christ.

Gracious God, known to us in Jesus Christ, revive your church so that we may bear faithful witness to you! Grant to its leaders the prophet's vision of that time when no infant lives but a few days, no one labors in vain, and even former enemies eat together. Grant to us the prophet's courage to stand fast when those around us dismiss such vision as utopian. Grant to us the prophet's zeal that we may demonstrate the credibility of your future by acting to make it so.

Through your Holy Spirit, protect your church from the sins of arrogance and complacency, and from the unjust use of power, that in all we say and do your name may be praised!

Amen.

MICHAEL KINNAMON, a Disciples of Christ minister, formerly professor of theology and peace studies at Eden Seminary, is General Secretary of the National Council of Churches of Christ in the U.S.A. A major ecumenical thinker and leader, he had previously served in both the National and World Councils of Churches and written several books on directions in ecumenical work.

For Freedom from the Idolatry
of Group Purpose

Lord, we thank you that you give us the chance to work in fellowship in many kinds of groups and organizations toward many shared purposes. We know that the thrill of cooperation and achievement can sometimes lead us astray. We pray for your forgiveness that we so regularly lower our eyes from the hills of glory and focus them on goals that advance the interests of the few over the needs of the many.

We ask you, whether we are at home or at work, to propel our hearts, our minds, and souls outward, away from small and narrow identities and toward the immense and eternal. For when our minds are small, we lose the awe with which to perceive the riotous wealth of your galaxy-bedazzled creation. When our hearts are small, our love cannot bridge the dark waters of suffering and brokenness. When our souls are small, we fall back behind the cruel and inhuman boundaries of our own making.

Through the life and death of Jesus, we have witnessed the all-healing force of your grace. Therefore, through the miracle of your spirit, lead us and all human groups beyond the narrow constraints of our vision, even and perhaps especially when we are motivated by faith, that we might forcefully and fearlessly seek mercy and justice for all. Whenever we stray toward idolatry of group purpose, whenever we seek the favor of approval of the few, draw us back in faithfulness to you.

Bring us to a gentle and complete awareness of our own limited days, not that we might fear their brevity but that we might celebrate each moment as one of abundance, mindful that all boundaries, even that of death, melt away before the

merciful song of the universe, the song, oh source of light
and life and love, that only you can sing.

Amen.

ROBERT KINLOCH MASSIE has played key roles in two important
movements — the struggle for justice in South Africa and the struggle
to prevent environmental degradation — while struggling himself with
serious medical threats traceable to a tainted blood transfusion. A
founder of C.E.R.E.S., a voluntary business and social sector group,
he has helped improve business codes of conduct related to limiting carbon emissions and lessening the "through-put" of industrial
processes.

That We May Be a More Faithful People

In the midst of an increasingly complex, diverse, and
morally challenging world, we are called to a sustained
practice of personal and shared discernment. Together we
pray for the heart and will to enter into discernment in
order to be a more faithful presence in the life of the wider
world:

God, Our Loving Creator —
You, Creator Spirit, who move within us, among us,
   beneath us, and beyond us —
You who gather us together —

In this new threshold time in your holy history,
When we know we are complicit
In the degradation of both soils and souls,
You still invite us, call us, again and again
To be your people — whole and holy,
To live in alignment with your deep creative joy.

We are called again and again
  to your truth
Called again and again
  to your justice
Called again and again
  to your more abundant life.

We, though called, are given no obvious path,
only the way—the practice of discernment—
in this complex, suffering, and wonder-full
  world.

So we pray for the will to claim
Pause and the art of Presence
in a busy and distracted world.
We pray for the capacity to recognize
shared silence as a political act of interdependence
in a society fractured by individualism.
We pray for the stilling of inner chatter.
We pray for
  seeing hearts,
  listening souls,
  informed minds,
  and the grace, the gift, of your in-sight.
We pray for the courage to respond to your calling,
because we long at the deep core of our souls
to become again and again a more faithful people.
Amen.

SHARON DALOZ PARKS is a member of the Society of Friends
(Quaker) and director of "Leadership for the New Commons," an ini-
tiative of the Whidbey Institute. Among others, her publications
include *Leadership Can Be Taught: A Bold Approach for a Complex World*
(2005); *Big Questions, Worthy Dreams: Mentoring Young Adults in Their
Search for Meaning, Purpose, and Faith* (2000); and co-authored, *Common
Fire: Leading Lives of Commitment in a Complex World* (1997).

For the Spirit

O God, whose Spirit continues to hover over our broken lives and world, let your just and loving Spirit descend upon us so that we may rise up as people of faith to do justice and love kindness and walk humbly with God.

In a world of despair and hopelessness confronted with a pandemic of HIV/AIDS and with so many other sources of sickness and misery, grant that we may be among those who advocate healthcare as a human right.

In a divided, dangerous, and deadly world of war and genocide, grant that we may join others to become peacemakers who work for peace and reconciliation.

In a world of greed and global capitalism, grant that we may be counted among those who confess our own materialism and seek alternative means for local, regional, and global cooperation.

In a world of ecological destruction of our planet earth, grant that we may find ways to control pollution and global warming, beginning with our own homes and country.

In a world of separation and difference, teach us how to form communities that value difference and to give thanks for the ways we can come together to celebrate our many cultural, racial, and religious customs.

O God, whose spirit continues to hover over our broken lives and world, be present to us as Jesus was present to those in need long ago. Teach us to live out his life and ministry through our own actions so that we may discover your Spirit among the least of your brothers and sisters and even in our own ordinary lives.

In the name of Jesus Christ we pray.

Amen.

LETTY RUSSELL was a longtime faculty member at Yale Divinity School and one of the world's foremost feminist theologians. The author of seventeen influential books, Russell moved beyond her writing to activism that modeled ways to build community in her ministries. As one of the most committed feminist theologians in the ecumenical and interfaith communities, she devoted her career to making it possible for women around the world to have a voice in theological discussions. (This prayer is among her last written works.)

That We May Be Called Into a Covenant of Life Together

Gracious God of Sovereign Love,
We give you thanks for the gift of this creation; for the blessings of earth, water, and sky; and for the creatures who inhabit it and make it teem with life. Grant us such a sense of the giftedness of creation that we are transformed by its beneficence. Help us through the rich offerings of your grace to call into question the desecrations of your covenant with the earth and with the peoples of the world.

We repent, O God, of our participation and complicity in the violations of each other. Save us from talk of freedom that covers domination, from a language of justice that hides exploitation, and from mouthing about equities that deepens inequality.

Make us loathe to support wars when we send other people's children to fight them. May our tongues cleave to the roofs of our mouths when we delight in the stock market's success with no concern for what it does to people whom it exploits. Make us suspicious of governments that privilege wealth and ignore the poor.

O God, fill us with a passion for the common good and for a justice founded upon it. Call us again to a covenant of life together. Let us dream of a world where children are born to hope, where work serves vocation, and where righteousness and justice cover the earth. In the meanwhile let us embody these dreams in our lives.

Through Jesus Christ, our Lord,

Amen.

TEX SAMPLE is the Robert B. and Kathleen Rogers Professor Emeritus of Church and Society at Saint Paul School of Theology in Kansas City, Missouri. Before his life as a teacher, he worked as an oil field roustabout, as a laborer and cab driver, as well as a Methodist pastor and ecumenical advocate. He is known for his books on popular culture, the working class, changing lifestyles, and new forms of worship.

For Businesses and the Investment Community

O Lord, whose love and passion for justice touches all parts of our personal lives and every corner of our planet, help us as we strive to manage our economic lives in ways that benefit your people and your planet.

Lord, too often we live in silos with our religious life separate from our corporate or personal financial lives. We act as if every business decision or investment choice is somehow guided by economic rules that have nothing to do with the Spirit that we ask to guide our personal lives. Help us break down these mental barriers, these artificial walls, and see that each and every aspect of our lives must be an open book to your Spirit.

We ask your guidance to manage and channel the affairs of global companies, small business, and microenterprises so that as they seek profit they seek with equal passion to preserve our environment and planet; to provide a just distribution of wealth that allow families to feed, clothe, and house themselves; to ensure they are honestly and ethically managed; and take our neighbors seriously whether they live down the street or live in India or Guatemala.

And, O God of justice, as we look at our pension funds, foundations, and investment firms as they invest trillions of dollars into companies around the globe, help us to discern that each and every act of investing is also a moral act, a social choice, for these monies support and advance business agendas sometimes at odds with an agenda of justice or an agenda that serves your planet. Open our eyes to see that the "flow of capital" can contribute to human suffering and oppression or the uplifting of the lives of your people.

Help us see these choices not as "financial decisions" that have nothing to do with your agenda, but choices that need to be made consistent with your love, compassion, and passion for justice. And let our faith guide our voices and power as investors to press global companies to work in ways that love mercy and do justice.

Let our dollars speak for our hearts.

Help us be whole people.

Amen.

TIMOTHY SMITH serves as director of Socially Responsive Investing and senior vice president at Walden Asset Management (Boston). Previously, he was director of the Interfaith Center on Corporate Responsibility, the primary organization guiding U.S. religious denominations and orders in the use of their investments for social change in South Africa and Central America and on a range of social issues. A theologically trained lay United Methodist, Smith is originally from Canada.

⟨⟨⟨⟩ ⟨⟩⟩

To Live So That All Human and Natural Life Can Flourish

Blessed Trinity,

We pray to your creative spirit of the universe, which gives us life.

We pray in the name of Jesus, our Messiah, who has opened to us your way and some of the mystery of your being.

We pray to the Spirit we call Holy that incarnates thy self in the struggles of our common life.

Thou hast given us so much in the beauty, splendor, and complexity of our world, of which we are a part and on which we depend.

Because of the wondrous grace of your outpouring, we dare to ask in thankfulness for an understanding of how our common life can nurture us as partially free beings. May we live our lives in order and purpose so that all human life can flourish and natural life be sustained and restored.

In the teaching of Jesus and the prophets, show us the way to organize our life in this land so that our citizens may enjoy human creativity and solidarity. May our schools, families, vocations, and organizations reflect thy will as they are reformed to maximize both human equality and freedom.

We pray that our foolish war will fail and that we will retreat from imperial pretension beyond our shores. In thy mercy spare the lives of all that can be saved from the terror of war. Give to us in thy new way, we pray, the blessings of a more modest republic where all our people live well and more freely honor thy name and will.

Amen.

RONALD H. STONE was the John Witherspoon Professor of Christian Ethics at Pittsburgh Theological Seminary, from which he retired in 2003. He served six years on the Advisory Council of Church and Society of the UPCUSA and six years on the Advisory Committee of Social Witness of the Presbyterian Church (U.S.A.), chairing task forces on faith and politics, and peacemaking, intervention, and terrorism. His most recent books are *Resistance and Theological Ethics* (edited with Robert Stivers, 2004) and *Prophetic Realism: Beyond Militarism and Pacifism* (2005).

For Communities of Resistance
and Solidarity

Stubborn, stalwart, subverting God,
justice-demanding, peace-hungering, world-loving God,
God who breathes and births through community,
God who takes on muscle and flesh through
    community,
God who makes the unseen visible through
    community,
Give us, we pray:

communities with the craftiness of Shiph'rah and
    Puah, who through holy subterfuge wrested
    Hebrew babies from Pharoah's murdering hand;

communities with the dogged devotion of Ruth, who
    followed her bitter beloved Naomi to a foreign land;

communities with the boldness of Abigail, who did not
    ask permission before heading off to make peace
    with her husband's enemy;

communities with the tenacity of Rizpah, who through
    a fierce vigil over her slain sons exposed a king's
    depravity;

communities with the gall of Nathan, who pointed his
    bony finger right up into power's face;

communities with the discipline of Daniel, who said no
    to the best that Babylon had to offer;

communities with the courage of Shadrach, Meshach,
    and Abed'nego, who refused to pledge their
    allegiance to empire;

communities with the fidelity of Jahzei'ah and
    Jonathon, who would not consent to put away
    their foreign wives and children;

communities with the keen perception of Anna and
    Simeon, who saw hope for the world in the arms
    of a brand-new mother;

communities with the anger of Jesus, who raged
    against abusive powers;

communities with the temerity of the Syrophoenician
    woman, who refused to let others define her;

communities with the self-scrutiny of Paul, who
    confronted discrimination in his own circles;

communities with the audacity of Silas, who sang out
    joy through prison cell bars;

communities with the imagination of John, who
    envisioned a new heaven and a new earth from
    his island exile;

stubborn, stalwart, subverting God, gift our
    communities
with craftiness,
with dogged devotion,
with boldness,
with tenacity,
with gall,
with discipline,
with courage,
with fidelity,
with keen perception,
with anger,

with temerity,
with self-scrutiny,
with audacity,
with imagination,

so that we may we be faithful, and more than that, so
that we may be strategic, effective, and powerful,
not for the sake of ourselves, but for the sake of
this aching world;

so that we may love, and more than that, so that we
may we live in solidarity with those we love,
claiming their daily struggles as our own;

so that our communities may be expressions of your
realm, of your will, of your heart here on earth.

Amen.

THE REV. CINDY WEBER, an ordained Baptist minister, is pastor of
Jeff Street Baptist Community at Liberty in Louisville, Kentucky.

6

PRAYERS FOR PEOPLE IN VARIOUS VOCATIONS AND CIRCUMSTANCES

That Children May Also Feed Your Sheep

Thank you, God, for our families, for food and for peace.

God, we want to feed your sheep. Help us to take care of other people, to give help to other communities.

Help us to see those who are hungry, those who are poor and sick, those who are homeless and suffering.

Help us to share what we have with those who need it: to feed the hungry, give shelter to the homeless, give clothes, money and animals to people who need them.

And help us to treat others the way they want to be treated.

Amen.

KATIE BLACKERBY WEIBLE, Director of Education at Actor's Theatre of Louisville, Kentucky, worked with children ages seven to ten during a summer Peace Camp at Covenant Community Church to create a prayer drama. The prayer above is a compilation of prayers voiced by second- and third-grade students attending Peace Camp. Weible helped the group brainstorm what they might communicate to God about making them aware of others in need. She then transcribed the oral prayers of the group and compiled them into one written prayer. During Peace Camp the prayer was dramatized, and the children created a series of tableaux (frozen pictures) with their bodies to depict those in need, reaching out to them and finding a sense of peace.

For Those Who Hold Power and Responsibility

Lord, who in Jesus Christ
    became the Servant of all,
Grant that I may seek not only to lead
    but also to follow.
Grant that I may seek not only to influence
    but also to be influenced.
Grant that I may seek not only to be heard
    but also to hear.
In my efforts to change others,
    may I also be changed by them.
In my efforts to teach others,
    may I also learn from them.
In my efforts to be a source of growth for others,
    may I also experience growth with them.
Humble God, empower me with your Holy Spirit
    for this day.
Receptive, may I absorb and reflect
    your humility in Jesus,
Attending with love
    to each person I encounter.

Thus may I recognize
and honor you in them.

PHILIP W. BUTIN is president of and professor of theology at San Francisco Theological Seminary. He served in youth and pastoral ministry for over twenty-five years.

For Immigrants Seeking a Better Life for Their Families

En esta hora de Dios clamamos por el alma de aquellos que murieron en esa troca. Dios nuestro, perdieron sus vidas por buscar una mejor vida para sus familias. Clamamos también, Dios Santo, que le des paz a las familias que se quedaron en México y sus otros países de origen. Clamamos, O Dios, para que la paz del cielo llene sus corazones y pueda permanecer con ellos la esperanza de que un día puedan verse allá en el cielo, donde los que murieron ya están contigo. Dios Santo, clamamos por cada uno de los inmigrantes que están en este país. Danos, O Dios, la paciencia para encontrar trabajo y poder ayudar a nuestras familias que se han quedado en México. Dios Santo, te pedimos en nombre de Jesús, que estés con ellos y que tu justicia se haga presente en cada uno de nosotros.
Amén.

In this hour of God, we plead for the soul of those who died in that truck. Dear God, they lost their lives while searching for a better life for their families. Also, we plead, Holy One, that you give peace to the families who stayed in Mexico and their countries of origin. We implore you, O God, that the peace of heaven be in their hearts and that the hope will remain that one day they will see each other in heaven, where they are with you. Holy God, we plead for every immigrant who is in this country. Give us patience, dear God, so that we will be able to find work and be able to help our families who have stayed in Mexico. Holy God, we make this supplication in the name of Jesus. We ask you to be with them and may your justice become a reality in each one of us.

Amen.

This prayer was found at the Exxon Truck Stop/Immigrant Memorial Site. Attributed to "Efrain," it offers an elegy to one of the worst immigrant tragedies in United States history. Nineteen immigrants died in May 2003 while bound for Houston. They had been left trapped in a truck trailer along the highway and suffocated in the searing Texas heat.

<hr>

For Immigrants and Day Laborers

O God,

Who art with us here on earth,

Hallowed be your name among those who hunger after daily bread, in spite of abundance and waste, throughout the global commonwealth.

Let your kingdom come for the millions of your children who migrate across deserts, barren hills, rivers, and artificial walls of separation, hoping only to reach a place where they may earn "with the sweat of their brow" a living wage to feed and educate their children left behind.

May your kingdom come, we pray, for those who are heavy laden inside the United States, bending their backs under the sun day after day, picking the food for our tables; and for those who toil long hours in the kitchen, behind walls, always in fear of police raids and deportation, while many of us sit comfortably in the front rooms of thousands of restaurants, all over the country; and for the hundreds of thousands of day laborers who undertake dangerous jobs all over the country with minimal, if any, protection by health and safety laws.

Let your will be done for the millions of displaced and exiled (in Jordan, Syria, and throughout the Middle East, mostly from Iraq) because of inhuman interventions from abroad and fanatical violence from inside; and also for those afflicted by violence in Colombia: the two million peasants displaced and exiled in their own country, and for the widows and orphans who mourn the violent death of their husbands and parents who had dared to become labor organizers, innocent victims of the insatiable appetite for land and power of the dominant groups, including some multinational corporations exploiting banana plantations, oil fields, coal mines, and water resources.

And do not let us fall in the temptation of believing the slogans of "globalization" about "the freedom of the market" and "the rising waves that lift all boats," while millions of your children drown all over the world in the raging seas of greed and arrogance.

Let your will be done, O God, here on earth!

Amen.

GONZALO CASTILLO-CARDENAS is emeritus professor of church and society and third world studies at Pittsburgh Theological Seminary. Since his retirement in 2004, Professor Castillo moved to Dallas, Texas, and travels once a year to his native Colombia, where he teaches two-week intensive courses in Christian Social Ethics from a Latin American perspective.

For Servanthood in Business

Dear God,

You give us the gifts we need to flourish, spiritually, physically and creatively. You have trusted us, corporately and individually, as we make our own paths in a world defined more and more by material things. We are pressed constantly to take time and energy away from loving and caring in order to succeed. Yet in entering your time we find true success in a synchronicity of spirit beyond tactics and techniques, a place where even tools reflect the qualities of good work.

The vast number of interconnections that are now part of our everyday lives make global partnerships possible in business as never before. Still, we toss aside the learning of raised awareness in order to take the path of greater profits. Guide us as we use these connections to strengthen the web of our world rather than build a web to entrap or win out over others. Protect us as we evolve to support and nurture our businesses and projects as infrastructure opportunities to foster a more balanced and healthy world into the future, a world even with some of your forgiving qualities.

Forgive us, God, when we focus on competition rather than the calm petition of honest prayer, which presumes that we do not have—nor need to have—all of the answers. It is when we see the freedom and the possibility in this that your prayers for us will be achieved. What a gift to be able to find in you a brainstorm partner! What a gift to share our concerns and find a course of action through communication with One who sees every side of the story, not just our side! Help us to celebrate that prayer is the ultimate creative exercise; that your answers come in our responsible proactivity, and the joys of your presence outweigh the sorrows we sometimes bring.

We strive for corporate social responsibility, yet even there fear to go beyond quantitative measures of our results. Help us to know the satisfaction that comes from setting the measurements aside. We trust that the courage to change direction—to risk small mistakes in order to create big visions—will bring its own rewards, in the shared and sacred knowing that is a quality of wholly living.

We have so many tools at our disposal. We are often overwhelmed with the day-to-day management. Help us to recognize the simplicity of praying for business, even when every piece of technology gives and takes away. Give us the imagination to guide technology to be a vehicle of shared success—of freeing us to seek our higher selves, and to do this in a community of coworkers, partners, and fellow pathfinders. We pray to live into those most personal of moments when our connection to you and to all creation is one and the same; when losing our self-interests and measures is finding our individual and corporate success.

Amen.

PATRICIA H. CHAPMAN is the principal of Stone Soup Marketing in New York, a research and consulting firm specializing in new product concepts and brand positioning. She also develops curriculum for youth and young adults, such as BibleLaureate©, bringing Christian connections in literature and culture into inventive lesson form. She served on the Social Creed study team of the Presbyterian Church (U.S.A.).

For Farmworkers Struggling for a Just Wage

Dios todo lo puede y está con nosotras y nosotros hasta el fin de nuestros días.

Dios está siempre en dondequiera que estemos y cuando lo necesitamos; Dios está con los que luchan en este mundo. Dios está cuando luchamos contra el mal, cuando pisotean nuestros derechos y nos golpean, cuando nos maltratan tratándonos como esclavas y esclavos. A Dios no le molesta acompañarnos a las cortes judiciales cuando reclamamos justicia. Dios hará que haya justicia. Si no en este mundo, habrá justicia cuando rindamos cuentas ante Dios Todopoderoso al final de nuestras vidas.

Dios es grande, generoso, y bondadoso con todas y todos los que luchamos por una vida digna. Dios nos dice, "ayúdate que yo te ayudaré," y nos da la sabiduría, la fortaleza, y la fuerza para seguir adelante cuando estamos cansados de la situación que vivimos. Nos anima el saber que cuando alguien nos golpea, nos humilla, Dios se siente golpeado y humillado. Sabemos que podemos contar con Dios, en las buenas y en las malas.

Debemos de agradecerle a nuestro Dios por tener la oportunidad de luchar por justicia para toda la humanidad. Especialmente al estar lejos de nuestros países, lejos de nuestras familias, trabajando largas horas para poder mantenernos y poder mandar ayuda a nuestras familias —esta es la hora de luchar con fe, con amor, sabiendo que Dios siempre nos protege. Este convencimiento nos ayudará a continuar nuestra lucha por la justicia.

Ante Dios todas y todos somos iguales: ricos y pobres. Pero en la tierra los ricos nos quitan a los pobres lo poquito que tenemos para hacerse más ricos con el sudor de los pobres, dejando a los pobres hundidos en la miseria. Los ricos creen que pueden gozar a costa del pobre; pero el pobre goza de Dios, quien está siempre entre los que no tienen privilegios. Esta necedad divina es más sabia que toda sabiduría humana; la debilidad divina es más fuerte que toda fortaleza humana.

El sufrimiento pone a prueba nuestra fe en Dios. A veces nos parece que Dios está ausente o se ha convertido en un incapaz. Pero tenemos que confiar que Dios esta siempre con los que luchan por la justicia.

¡Qué Dios nos cuide, nos guarde, y nos bendiga!
Amen.

God is almighty and is with us and lives with us every day until the end.

The Lord is always wherever we are and is with all the struggles throughout the world. When we are struggling against evil, when our rights are trampled, when we are beaten or mistreated, even enduring conditions of slavery every day, the Lord is not angered when the people responsible for these conditions are taken to court to bring about justice.

God will bring justice, and though it may not be the justice of humankind on earth, we will have to stand before God almighty at the end of our lives and be judged.

God is great, generous, and kind with us who struggle for a life with dignity for all. God says, "Help yourself that I will help you" for a reason. God gives us the wisdom and the strength to continue forward when we are tired of our situation.

Because when someone beats you or humiliates you, in reality they are not only beating you or humiliating you, they are doing this to our God almighty, whom we are with in the good and the bad.

That is why we must be thankful to God when we are in any struggle for justice for humanity. Especially when we are far from our country, far from our family, working long hours to be able to sustain ourselves and to help our families. We arrived here for a reason, and now it is time to fight with faith, love, and hope in our Savior that always protects us. This is how we will continue forward in the struggle for justice.

God made everyone equal. God did not make rich and poor; humans on earth have created inequities, making themselves richer from the sweat of the poor and leaving them drowning in misery. The rich believe they can rejoice at the expense of the poor; but the poor rejoice in God who is always present amidst those without privilege. This divine foolishness is wiser than any human wisdom. God's weakness is stronger than all human strength.

The faith in God almighty can be tested by experience and suffering. Sometimes it seems that God is absent and incapable, but we must know that God is always where there is justice.

May God take care of us, protect us, and bless us.
Amen.

FRANCISCA CORTES, a Zapotec Indian from Oaxaca, Mexico, is a farmworker and member of the CIW. When Francisca was eighteen she immigrated to the United States in order to help send her younger brothers and sisters to school. After experiencing firsthand the injustices and miserable wages in the southwest Florida tomato fields, she joined with the Coalition of Immokalee Workers to fight for better wages and treatment for her fellow workers (www.ciw-online.org). A nationally respected speaker and grassroots leader, in 2005 she was a finalist for the Cardinal Bernadin Award for young leaders. A practicing Catholic, Francisca resides in Immokalee, Florida.

<hr />

By and For Teenagers

Dear God,

You have given our generation daily contact with others very different from ourselves. We sit in classrooms, play sports, and chat on the Internet with a much more diverse group than any generation before ours. On the one hand, we take diversity for granted. On the other, we still feel and act with stereotypes and judgments that limit what we can learn and share with one another as we grow into the wider world with our peers.

Please guide us to see past the physical, social, and cultural differences; not to be blind to them, but to accept them. Help us to remember that each of us is an individual with unique gifts, personal dreams, and value to the group. Too often, we react with laughter or teasing when we see the unique side of others, for it makes them "different." We react with anger and attitude when teachers and parents tell us what to do, feeling that we have earned some respect from them that is not always received. It is not easy to walk in someone's shoes or have others criticize the steps you've taken. It is not easy to find the balance between acting for others and gaining wisdom for ourselves. Nor is it always easy to see the difference in those actions that are self-confident and those that are merely selfish. Give us the understanding to judge others by what is in their hearts, and the patience to forgive should others misjudge us.

We spend most of our time in schools and activities where religion is not in the curriculum, prayer is not in the schedule, and we may not think of you at all. We give thanks that you are there always, even if we come and go. Open our minds to an attitude of mutual respect that we may listen and learn from those who see the world through different lenses, different stages of life, or different hurts and heritages. Open our hearts to let in your healing and strength and understanding when life is overwhelming. Give us the courage to help our friends do the same.

We want to enjoy a world where following our own path in life does not take away from our communities but gives back for a healthier world, in earth and in spirit. We want to know a world where diversity is a teacher and a guide, not an obstacle to community and a reason for exclusion, mockery, and hate. We want to give freely towards the future and to believe that it will be good. Through your love and guidance, we can work together — as we must work together — to make it so.

Amen.

ALEXANDER D'ATTORE and brothers RYAN and ERIC SCHUSTER are members of the Scarborough Presbyterian Church BibleLaureate© program and are students in Ossining, New York. Youth advisors are Joel Cambron and Patricia Chapman.

For Children

Lord, you came to us as a baby, poor, far from home, born to a young mother, your life in jeopardy from the beginning.

We claim to worship you, yet we fail to see you in children today, especially those who bear the heavy burden of poverty on small shoulders.

We fail to see you in children without homes to call their own, silent in the vain hope that the problem will just go away. We imagine that these, your children, don't feel our disdain that crawls like bugs and rats over their young bodies, don't feel our harsh indifference that penetrates to the bone like the cold drafty shelter, as they accustom themselves to the chaos and insecurity that darken their lives like an apartment whose lights have been cut off.

We fail to see you in children born to children themselves yearning for love from boyfriends and babies, having found too little in their families and faith.

We fail to see you in children, especially black and Latino children, who are swept along the cradle-to-prison pipeline; are denied health care and the opportunity and support of good schools, strong families, and caring communities; are sucked into the undertow of a culture that glorifies violence, expects little of them, and passes injustice onto another generation.

Hold us to account, O God, for our treatment of your children. Make us tremble to withhold our compassion and voice from your most vulnerable; to hate you by hating your beloved children.

Open our eyes, Lord. Help us to recognize you in *every* child, not just our own but the ones least like "our own." Help us to love you by loving all the children you have given us as a sacred trust.

Instill in us your vision and help us to proclaim it and live it. Fix our sights on the justice you intend for all children, especially those who are poor, abused, and in greatest jeopardy. Move us to create a world in which every child's basic survival needs are met: food, shelter, protection, health care, good schools, safety, family. Move us to create a world in which all children have what they need to thrive: love, hope, joy, faith. Help us open to all children the rich world of books and music and art, and the purpose of service and sharing and caring. Help us weave communities in which all children feel connected to caring others, in which our diversity is celebrated and our shared identity as your beloved children is affirmed.

Help your beloved children, O God, see themselves as precious in your sight. Grant that they may come to know your love and justice despite, if not because of, what we your people do. Instill in each of them an unwavering confidence that they are loved by you. In your tender mercy, grant that every child may live the life which you intend.

This we ask in the name of Jesus, that baby born so long ago and the one who seeks to live in our hearts today. Amen.

MARIAN WRIGHT EDELMAN, Baptist and related to many preachers, is founder and president of the Children's Defense Fund in Washington, DC. She is a longtime champion of justice for children, a well-known speaker and author, and an effective advocate before Congress.

For Saints

Dear God,

Who planted in our hearts the yearning for happiness, the longing for peace, the desire to love; thank you for the example of your saints, both those who are recognized and those who are obscure, the great "cloud of witnesses" who have gone before and who surround us still, who support us by their prayers and by their example, who have dared us to live more faithfully, more generously, and more courageously.

Help us to know their stories, their moments of weakness and doubt as well as their victories; let them become our true friends and companions, so that we too may respond as they did to the voice that calls us to go farther, to go deeper into the heart of our vocation; to conform our hearts to the pattern of the gospel.

Your saints remind us that there is a path to holiness that lies within our individual circumstances, that engages our own talents and temperaments, that contends with our own strengths and limitations, that responds to the needs of our own neighbors and our particular moment in history. They teach us that we don't need to be in a monastery or a chapel to find the path to your will, which lies in each situation, each encounter, each task before us.

Help us to begin today, this moment, where we are, to add to the balance of love in the world, to add to the balance of peace, so that your will may be done on earth as it is in heaven.

Amen.

ROBERT ELLSBERG is the publisher of Orbis Books in Maryknoll, New York. His own works include *All Saints: Daily Reflections on Saints, Prophets, and Witnesses for Our Time* (1997). He has edited many award-winning books and has broadened the Orbis list to include the major twentieth-century spiritual writers; Gandhi, Weil, Merton, and many less known. He has recently edited the journals of Dorothy Day.

For Parents

Gracious God,

We give thanks to you for the blessing and privilege of being parents. Help us to embrace parenthood as a sacred trust, giving to all parents a sense of wonder and awe for the gift of their children. May your love enable us to embrace the joys that children bring to our lives and give to us the resources of patience, wisdom, and faith to handle the responsibility of raising children. Enable us to celebrate the growth and maturity of our children, allowing us to rejoice in our children's accomplishments while also embracing their struggles, disappointments, and pains.

In times of doubt and frustration, provide us an open ear and heart to listen to our children's voices before raising our own voices. Amidst our frustration and anxiety when we question our ability as parents, give us the reassurance that you bless us, as we ourselves are a blessing to our children. Provide us the ongoing wisdom to discern how best to nurture our children, leading them on the road to adulthood. Enable us to guide our children to maturity and to send them out into the world filled with confidence and faith.

We give thanks for the diversity of people who are called to be parents. Remind us that the gift of parenthood comes to all kinds of people from different lifestyles and cultures who share a common bond to love and nurture children. May you give to all parents the ability to model the gifts of humility, compassion, and love that bespeak the presence of your own perfect love manifested in our homes and in our hearts.

Loving God, we pray for those who long to be parents yet find through no fault of their own that this gift is elusive. Remind us that the responsibility for the care of children is for everyone in our society. Encourage us to become models of discipleship to all children, in our families, churches, and communities. In words and deeds, may the church affirm its unconditional love for children as a sacred part of the body of Christ, and may the church be a place where parents experience a renewing and supportive fellowship sustained by the miracle of your grace.

In lifting up the gifts of parenthood and for the ways that the church is called to assist us in the care of children, we give thanks in Christ's name.

Amen.

CHRISTOPHER H. EVANS is Sallie Knowles Crozer Professor of Church History at Colgate Rochester Crozer Divinity School. He has done extensive research on the social gospel movement and is the author of *The Kingdom Is Always But Coming: A Life of Walter Rauschenbusch* (2004) and editor of *The Social Gospel Today* (Westminster John Knox, 2001). An ordained United Methodist minister, he has published extensively in the areas of American religious history, theology and popular culture, and ministry studies.

For the World's Children

How long, O Lord? How long will children suffer and die? How long will babies be born for calamity and mothers mourn?

Tens of thousands of children die needlessly each day, O God. Why don't you save them? Why don't we? Small children are sent far from home to toil for others, guns are thrust into the hands of little ones told to act like men, young bodies are exploited for adult gain; they are like prey in the jaws of wild dogs. Hunger stalks the children; illness and death lurk as malnutrition weakens the children. When they can no longer outrun their pursuers—the warfare, disease, tainted water, injustice—they falter and death pounces, ripping to shreds their hope, their potential, their families, their very lives.

Our children are in the pit, O God. They languish out of our sight, where no one hears or heeds their cries. They are numbered among the dead, even when they yet have life in them. They have been forgotten by most of us; we are unconcerned in our world of excess, distracting ourselves if we feel despair, dulling our feelings of helplessness and hopelessness with diversions.

Wake up, O God! Wake us up! We cannot slumber through the injustice; we cannot sleep through the suffering. It's time to do something about this! Bring your justice, O God. Bring your compassion. Save the children; help *us* save the children and save our souls.

Our children do not deserve to suffer. No child should feel the cruel blows of hunger, servitude, or warfare. No child should bear the burden of burying parents, raising siblings, and fending for herself.

You used midwives and mothers, the oppressed and the privileged, to save the baby Moses; help us save our children now. You used Moses to bring the children of Israel out of bondage; help us save our children now. You showed the starving people in the desert how to find manna and taught them not to hoard more than they needed; help us save our children now. You heard the cry of the child Ishmael and lifted his mother from despair; help us save our children now.

But you do see, and you do care. Your heart is the first to break when a little one suffers and dies. Your heart is the first to break when you see our indifference and injustice. Even though we fail each other, we can trust in you whose love fails not.

We will praise you for the wonder of children you have entrusted to our care, for the passion for justice that may course through our veins, for the compassion that beats in our hearts. We will praise you with our words and our work, with our hearts and our hands.

SHANNON DALEY-HARRIS is a religious organizing consultant, editor, and author of many liturgical resources for families and children. A Presbyterian, she was director of Religious Affairs at the Children's Defense Fund and developed many elements of the Children's Sabbath Program.

For a Teacher

Dear Lord, I thank you for placing me in this worthy profession of educating children. I believe in your Word, which is your expressed will for my life. I pray that your plan for my life will be accomplished as I submit myself in love to you. With gratitude, I join others who have answered your call to teach and now work with such dedication, ability, and care in our schools.

Lord, I pray that you will help me awaken hope for all children, especially children with special needs. Help me to see the great potential in each student and to learn from the children trust and forgiveness. Help me, I pray, to live in the present and to know that the future is in your hands.

Grant me, O Lord, I pray, wisdom, patience, and the grace to meet the challenge each day. Help me keep in mind in all that I do that while my students may be neglected, abandoned, and abused, as your children they deserve a quality education and need to feel your presence as seen by my actions. Fill me with a sense of protection, justice, and compassion. In the midst of the day, please help me bring joy and laughter and make life with its problems a bit easier to face.

Heavenly God, I know you are strong. Give me strength to remain steadfast and faithful in service. I thank you for choosing me as your own child. I trust you to lead and guide me through your Word with the Holy Spirit as my helper.

Lord, I give you all the glory and the praise.

Amen.

CARRIE HARRIS is an elder in the Presbyterian Church and currently serves on the Committee on Social Action's Social Creed Task Force. Carrie is recently retired after serving forty years as a professional school counselor and district administrator. She holds BS and MEd degrees from the University of Memphis. She and Jim, her husband, are members of Liberation Community Presbyterian Church, Memphis, Tennessee.

⸎⸎⸎

For Those Without a Place to Call Home

Spirit of new life,
Breathe into our fragmented communities
with your great imagination.

Awaken our desires and dreams
to live our lives centered in your covenant.

You, like your people,
have felt what it is to wander.
You have felt what it is to be left
without a place to call home,
to live as an outcast
with a longing and hope for a better world.

You have also reminded us,
through the stories of Hagar, Job, Naomi, Jonah,
and Dinah,
through the stories of those who have lost their
own sense of identity and worth,
through the stories of those without a home of
their own,
through the stories of those who have fled their
homes as refugees,
that you hear us when we are most vulnerable,
and travel with us in our greatest times of need.

We have drawn artificial boundaries and borders
to build up our egos,
to keep people out,
to protect our individual and national interests.

Those boundaries give us the false assurance
that we can hold on to our own identities,
that we can hold on to our own prosperity
as if we are not connected to others.

Many of us seek to define ourselves
by competing with others,
trying to gain wealth or authority
that will set them apart.

Yet neither wealth nor authority really tell us
    who we are.
We are too often left wandering, wondering,
and despairing in valleys of insufficiency.

We have left others wandering through no choice
    of their own:
the homeless who sleep on park benches
as we turn our heads away;
refugees of war who have been plodding
toward a place of greater promise
to find only camps full of peril
and empty of the very things they need to survive.
Left without a nation to call their own,
their families are vulnerable,
their children shrunken to skin and bones.

Where, O God, is your greater vision?
Where, O God, is community?
Compassion?
Justice?
Loving-kindness?

You have given us the means.
Help us find a way.
Shatter individualism.
Gather us in as a community.
Enable us to find room for everyone at the inn.

Come again to revive our concern for others;
come again to give voice to those who have been
silenced in every corner of the earth.
Strengthen those communities that
already work to provide hospitality
to the strangers in our midst.

Open the eyes of others
to become communities of your compassion.

Put flesh on the bones of our community
so we will feel for one another;
cover them with sinews that will
power our work to build a new community;
restore the rhythm of our hearts to your
compassion and justice;
give us attentive ears to hear the sound of
your own heart beating.
Breathe new life and imagination into
the dry bones of our community,
and make the compassion and justice of your
covenant live within us again.

May it be.

ELIZABETH HINSON-HASTY is a minister of Word and Sacrament in
the Presbyterian Church (U.S.A.) and assistant professor of theology
at Bellarmine University. She is often called on to speak in churches on
issues concerning faith and public life. Her most recent book is *Beyond
the Social Maze: Exploring Vida Dutton Scudder's Theological Ethics* (2006).

For Many, Many, Many Women

Lord, we come before you once again to ask your
    blessings upon the many, many women of this
    world who struggle to bring meaningful and fulfill-
    ing lives to their families — particularly the needs of
    the children they nurture.
There are many, many women who —
    gather ill-fed children to their breast that are
    depleted of sustenance because they themselves

have not received sufficient nutrients in their meager diets.

We beg your blessing upon them. . . .

There are many, many women who—
  carry their children to separation barriers, barbed
  wire fences and concrete walls in search of health
  care for their children only to be turned away with
  no care given at all or delayed at best.

We beg your blessings upon them. . . .

There are many, many women who—
  will face their first Mother's Day without a child, a
  child who has been lost to war in some faraway
  nation that they themselves may never see.

We beg your blessings upon them. . . .

There are many, many women who—
  will flee bands of raiders that seek to rape and
  humiliate them only to prove what they believe is
  their superiority over another family of your people.

We beg your blessings upon them. . . .

There are many, many women who—
  alone piece together limited resources to educate
  their children so that the entire family may someday
  have a life that is abundant with the necessities of
  living fruitfully.

We beg your blessings upon them. . . .

There are many, many women who—
  suffer physical, mental, and emotional humiliation
  at the hands of those who originally vowed to

honor, cherish and love them in marriage vows
both given and received.

We beg your blessings upon them. . . .

There are many, many women who—
find that they have happily conceived a child when
desired; yet others who unexpectedly conceive and
must make decisions about an unintended pregnancy.

We beg your blessings upon them . . .

Lord, again we pray for the many, many women who
are often the brunt of the ills of all societies—both
rich and poor. Give these women the strength to
persevere, the fortitude of steadfastness, and a wisdom of what could be a more-sustaining life that is
full with the security and acknowledgment your
wisdom brings to help us all to find our way out of
no way.

THE REV. ELENORA GIDDINGS IVORY served as director of the
Washington Office of the Presbyterian Church (U.S.A.) from 1989 to
2007. The Washington Office is the public policy information and
advocacy office of the Presbyterian Church (U.S.A.). Reverend Ivory
continues her work on human rights issues internationally at the World
Council of Churches in Geneva, where she is director of Public Witness: Addressing Power and Affirming Peace.

For People Who Are Homeless

Hungry are we, O God of the oppressed, for justice.

Thirsty are we, O God of liberation, for human rights.

We come before you on this day-for-free,
O creator,
that you are making
in the midst of the empire's weapons
of mass distraction

We come
to focus,
to commit,
to act,
to struggle,
to fight,
to love,
to shout as loud as we can,
to wage peace

for your abandoned ones
who wander the mean streets
with nowhere to go
in this nation at war
with Iraq, at itself.

You Companion of Compassion
who dearly love
beggars & prostitutes,
children fighting rats under bridges,
starving mothers whose milk cannot nourish,
prisoners who sit in abandoned hell holes,
without the visits that your son commands.

You who
come to us in the stranger's guise as
drunks and addicts,
widows and orphans,
beggars in velvet,
mumblers and incoherent poets of your word of fire,
lost lawless lawyers whose bar code is: Out,
teachers who dared to tell the way the truth the life,
veterans who fought our wars abroad
& have no homes in their homeland (no security, no
    patriots' act for them).

You, O God of justice,
cry out
like a woman alone in childbirth:

"Housing is a human right
Go tell it on the mountain,
in the sanctuaries,
on the streets,
at the courthouses and the halls of congress,
House my People today,
I say,
in the fierce urgency of now.

Woe to you prosperity preachers.
Woe to you blind, cruel police
who hurt and harm my unhoused.

Woe to those who own two houses while I sleep
     in a barn.
Woe to the rich while I suffer from poverty.
Woe to the well-fed while I stand in the soup line.
Woe to those who cheer for tax cuts while
     my people have no where to go but jail."

Help help help
us not simply to endure.
Grant us the strength to build the beloved community
     on earth;
to carry on with love & struggle & sacrifice
     in the streets.

Grant us dignity
as we build a destiny of righteousness & justice,
of love & peace,
of equality and housing for all,
of human rights.

In the name of the one who lifted Dr. Martin
     Luther King Jr.
to be the brightest light of this nation

as he followed in the footpaths of Jesus, the Human
   One.
And as King confessed with his back against the wall:
"But amid all of this we have kept going with
   the faith
that as we struggle, God struggles with us
& that the arc of the moral universe, although long,
is bending toward justice."

In the names of
Abraham and Sarah,
Yahweh-Elohim,
Allah,
Jesus, the Human One,
Harriett Tubman,
Martin & Malcolm,

Amen.

EDUARD "The Agitator" LORING is a Presbyterian minister and a
co-founder of the Open Door Community in downtown Atlanta, Georgia. Married to Murphy Davis, he is a street preacher in the tradition
of John the Baptist. He visits the prisoner and gives hell to the political
and business community which wants to shut the homeless out of
Atlanta—a "sacrilege" against the Beloved Community of Jesus the
Christ, Martin Luther King Jr., you, and me.

For Intelligence Analysts

Gracious God,
   We pray for those entrusted to tell the truth to our
country's leaders so that they can make fully informed
decisions. Your Word assures us, "You shall know the
truth, and the truth shall set you free." That verse from
John's Gospel is chiseled into the white marble entrance to
the Central Intelligence Agency. Sadly, this ethos is in
jeopardy, as our country gravitates ever closer to Caesar's
cynical quip "What is truth!"

Honest intelligence analysts have become an endangered species. Give them the courage to ply their trade with assurance that your abiding Spirit never goes off duty.

Our Judeo-Christian heritage gives us insight into your God's-eye vision of justice. Clearly, your vision is a far cry from that symbolized by the familiar image of a woman blindfolded to indicate a complete lack of bias. Thank you for helping us see that your brand of justice is biased and prejudiced to the core in favor of what the Bible calls the *anawim*—the hated, despised poor; the widow, orphan, stranger; the people we try not to notice on the sidewalks of our inner cities and outside bombed-out homes in war-torn lands. Your Word points the way toward implementing that biblical vision of justice, but—strange God that you are—you decided to depend on us; and—stranger still—you gave us the freedom to do justice, or not. Help us to do it.

We pray often for peace; help us to pray more often for justice, for we know from your Word that peace is nothing more nor less than the experience of justice; and that injustice is often a vast swamp breeding violence.

Since the pursuit of justice and peace is condemned to failure without truth, we urgently ask that you give our intelligence analysts the courage to speak truth to power, as your prophets did of old—no matter the cost to career or even to livelihood. May they act always in the knowledge that without truth there can be no justice; and without justice there can be no peace.

When they deal with wars and rumors of war, give them the strength to thwart any pressures to trim their analysis to the winds blowing from the offices of leaders not always wanting to hear the unvarnished truth.

Help intelligence analysts, instead, always to look through the wider lens of your justice and peace, to seek the truth on which both must be based, and then to tell it. And should they become aware of decisions for illegal attacks on other countries, give them the courage to honor their duty to you, and to our Constitution, to find ways to make the truth available to fellow citizens unable to learn it in any other way.

RAY MCGOVERN received the Central Intelligence Agency's distinguished service award after twenty-seven years of service, which included briefing Presidents Nixon, Carter, Ford, Reagan, and G. H. W. Bush. He is a leader in Veteran Intelligence Professionals for Sanity, writes frequently on foreign affairs, and works with Tell the Word, a ministry of The Church of the Saviour in Washington, DC.

A Lawyer's Prayer

Creator, Most Holy Judge,

I come before you with thanksgiving for the call to serve you in the halls of justice with the blessed assurance that every person is my neighbor.

I am grateful to you for those who seek my counsel.

As advisor, I pray for competence and for words to impart understanding of rights and obligations as my clients seek a light for their path to a perfect day.

As an advocate, I pray that in my zealousness, I am mindful always of the rules and traditions by which I am to be guided in the adversary system. All the while, in living by my faith, I ask for the wisdom and courage to make changes needed for a more just world.

As a negotiator, may my quest for my client's advantage not be at the expense of honest dealing with others.

As an intermediary, I pray for the ability to instill a
desire for justice and a love for mercy in those who
struggle and are in conflict, so that they can begin
their walk on the path of reconciliation with each
other and with God.

In my labor, Lord, make me an instrument of thy will:
to seek power for the powerless, to serve the less
fortunate, to speak for those whom Jesus taught me
to love by his example.

May the fruit of my labor for justice bring peace to the
homes of those I am blessed to serve and to this
world you love.

Amen.

LIDIA SERRATA LEDESMA is a pioneering Mexican American lawyer
in Victoria, Texas. Starting as a social worker, she soon shifted to law,
and has combined both private practice and public involvement
throughout her career. She is also an Elder at Iglesia Nicea Presbiteri-
ana, Victoria, Texas, and has served on study task forces of the Presbyterian Church (U.S.A.), including as chair of its resolution team on a
Social Creed for the Twenty-First Century,

For Mothers

In the beginning was the Word
and the Word was with God
and the Word was God
and She was known as Sophia.

Present at the beginning of creation
you blew breath into our very souls;
groaning in travail, you gave birth to creation.
God, our Mother, hear our prayer.

Rejoice with us in the pleasure of our joys:
for mothers
    who sing lullabies and rock songs to soothe
        and entertain their babies,
    who play endless games of Hi Ho CherryO
        and Chutes and Ladders,
    who braid hair, potty-train, cook, clean,
        and do laundry,
    who learn something new about what it means
        to love by being a mother.
Mother God, the delight of our children fills
    our hearts and our souls with joy.
We give thanks for the myriad ways that they bless
    our lives and communities.

Weep with us in the pain of our laments:
for mothers who bleed
    from abortions of unwanted or impossible
        pregnancies,
        from rape and assault,
            from domestic violence and homicide.
We need better birth control, sex education,
    and a transformation of our culture of violence.
We pray for the will and the strength to get involved
    in facilitating this transformation.

For mothers who cry
    when they can't make their rent,
        when their children go hungry,
            when they lose their children to drugs,
                prison, or gang violence,
we need affordable housing, social safety nets,
    and community alternatives for idle teens.
Help us commit ourselves and our churches to
    making these changes in our local communities.

For mothers who have had enough
of asthma attacks and hospital rooms when
there is no insurance,
of losing jobs for staying home with a sick child,
of low-wage, dead-end jobs,
we need universal health coverage and new ways
of envisioning work and life.
We ask for imagination and the political courage
to make this a reality.

For mothers who are lonely, tired, hateful, loving,
energetic, absent, overbearing, fun, silly, sad,
courageous, ill, angry, soft-spoken, old, young,
and in-between;
for women who mother their own children or the
children of others;
for adopted moms, and birth moms,
and single moms and grand moms;
for the moms we had and the moms we want to be —
we thank you, O God, our Mother.

Help us to remember that no one mothers in isolation
and that all mothers need support, courage,
assistance, and friendships to make it through.
Help us remember what it means to be communities
of Christ in the world,
and help us work to support mothers in our
communities and in our nation.

Amen.

REBECCA TODD PETERS is associate professor of religious studies at Elon University. She is an ordained PC(USA) minister and is currently serving as a member of the Faith and Order Commission of the World Council of Churches. Her book *In Search of the Good Life: The Ethics of Globalization* (2004) won the 2003 Trinity Book Prize. She has also coedited two books, *Justice in the Making* (2004) and *Justice in a Global Economy: Strategies for Home, Community and World* (2006).

Psalm of a Low-wage Worker

Beloved
Mother, Father,
Sister, Brother,
Source of all creation,

Thank you for the gift of life,
for the *"beloved community,"*
realized each time
we make concrete your love and justice;
renewed each time
we recognize *you* in ourselves,
and in the eyes of each other and in those we serve;
fulfilled each time
we are recognized in the fullness of our humanity
with dignity and respect.

God of Love and Justice,
we are workers,
teachers and homecare workers,
hospital and service workers,
daycare providers and firefighters,
technical workers and farm workers,
factory workers and janitors,
day laborers and office workers,
immigrants and descendants of immigrants,
slaves and descendants of slaves,
bound together across borders
with common dreams —

dreams of home, hearth, health, safety, community;
food for the body, mind, and spirit;

time to reap the fruits of our labor;
well-being for ourselves, our families, our neighbors,
   our world.

We seek
the right not only to survive but to thrive,
the right to participate and to be heard,
the opportunity to imagine and create the future.

We lay claim
to our rightful place at the table
and the exercise of economic citizenship,
blessed by the blood of all who have come before and
all who come after us in the struggle for respect
   and recognition.

We lift our collective voice
and declare:
The economy exists for all people, not the few;
people do not exist for the economy!

The well-being of our families is inextricably bound
with the well-being of yours;
your freedom intertwined with ours;
our past and futures woven together in the air
   we breathe,
the water we drink, the clothes we wear, the land
   we share,
the children we raise, the languages we speak,
the hopes and dreams we carry, the divine spark
   within!

God of Compassion and Light,
grant us courage to continue the struggle.
Grant us hope born by coming together in love,
   with power for justice.

Accompany us as we join together with our coworkers
　　near and far,
asserting our right for
　　a place at the table,
　　a better future for all;
asserting the right to organize,
　　the right to unionize,
　　the moral imperative to set ourselves free!

Take our hands as we take each other's hands
and unearth the promised land—the *"beloved*
community"—on this earth as in heaven.
Amen.

EILEEN PURCELL is a senior staff member at the Service Employees'
International Union, charged with reviving church-labor solidarity.
She is the former executive director of the SHARE Foundation and a
cofounder of the Sanctuary Movement for Central American refugees
and the National Sanctuary Defense Fund (NSDF) during the 1980s.
She has worked in defense of international human rights and with
immigrants and political refugees from Central America, Mexico,
Argentina, and Chile for more than twenty-five years.

For Those in Statecraft
and International Relations

Sovereign Lord,
　　We pray for the people who are charged with representing our nation as they bridge culture, race, and religion to
painstakingly negotiate terms of trade and forge alliances
of security. May they view their task as sacred and be filled
with hope, creativity, and endurance so that the bonds they
forge among nations may bring mutual benefit and lasting
peace. Lord, help our leaders to look beyond grand palaces
and corporate offices to consider carefully the effects that

the policies they are creating will have on the humble homes of average citizens. May America be girded by the spirit of cooperation and generosity that recognizes the needs of others alongside our own so that the entire world might enjoy a common wealth of food, drink, shelter, education, and recreation.

Lord, may America not succumb to imperial temptations; rather, through persons of character, remind us of our shared religious heritage of servanthood. May we use our power in concert with the international community so that we might together bring in a new era marked by justice and peace. Let restraint and compassion stay the cruel hand of war that slays the young and leaves societies broken and bloody. May cool minds prevail in seasons hot with destructive cycles of revenge. In combating the evils of this day let us not become what we despise. Rather, hold us fast to our conviction that living without intimidation or deprivation is a human right for other nations as well as ourselves.

God of the Universe, when we forsake the hubris of claiming you as our private possession, may we feel the freedom of your claim on us as we work for reconciliation and the common good. Lord, may none use religion as a rallying call for national militarism, territorial expansion, or terror based on idolatrous readings of sacred texts. Let us instead recognize the sacred in other human beings from every nation, class, race, or religion. Help us to love both you and our neighbor and thereby fulfill the great commandment of your Son Jesus Christ, so that through our efforts for peace we might be known as your children.

May America and the entire world be blessed by your continued providence even in the struggles of the future. May thy kingdom come, thy will be done throughout the earth as it is in heaven.

Amen.

THE REV. PAUL BRANDEIS RAUSHENBUSH is the associate dean of religious life and the chapel at Princeton University. Raushenbush is a contributing editor for Beliefnet.com; the author of *Teen Spirit: One World, Many Faiths* (2006); and the editor of the hundredth-anniversary edition of his great-grandfather Walter Rauschenbusch's book *Christianity and the Social Crisis—In the 21st Century* (2007). He is the codirector of the Program on Religion, Diplomacy and International Relations at the Liechtenstein Institute on Self-Determination at Princeton University.

<hr>

For Child Workers

Blessed are you, Creator of the universe. Look with compassion on all your children: those who play free of worry and want, and those who know nothing of ease and fullness. We beseech you in your tender mercy to help us see the silent tears and hear the muffled cries of the millions of child workers in our world.

O God of many names, we pray for Rosa, a little girl who sells flowers on the busy streets of Mexico City; for Saheed, a ten-year-old boy who runs machinery in a filthy, hot factory in Calcutta; for Darunee, a thirteen-year-old girl who is caught in the sex trade in Thailand; for Santos, a sixteen-year-old migrant field worker in the United States; for Julia, an eight-year-old domestic worker in the Philippines; and for all the children who work long days and nights in dangerous, life-stunting, and dream-destroying conditions. Forgive us, O Lord, for our lack of awareness of these children's situation, for our complicity in and indifference to the effects of a global economy—too often driven by greed, lust, and profit—on the world's child workers.

Embolden us, as your people, to speak out against the evil of child labor, and to work with faith communities, corporations, international agencies, and governments for the liberation and protection of children from cruel working conditions and from lives that hold little or no hope. O

God, shine the lantern of your love and light upon these precious children. Watch over them and bless them. Illumine our hearts and minds with the realization that every child worker is our child, a child of your universe, and a member of one great family.

Amen.

DR. DIANNE REISTROFFER is an ordained minister in the United Methodist Church. She currently serves as professor of ministry and director of Methodist studies at Louisville Presbyterian Theological Seminary. Dr. Reistroffer co-teaches a course titled Child Advocacy in the Church and sits on several boards of nonprofit organizations dedicated to the welfare and rights of children. She has also engaged in short-term mission work with children in India and Bangladesh.

For Prisoners

O God, you who are the hope of the hopeless and the One by whose grace all imprisoned spirits know true freedom, we beseech your special care for persons who are constrained by all manner and means of incarceration.

We pray for those who have been beaten down by life and who, in desperation, have committed grievous crimes for which they are now remorseful. As they await sentencing, give them the fortitude to face punishment and the firmness of mind to use the time of incarceration to secure a renewed sense of self-worth and a determination to contribute to our society's common good.

For those who have not been successful in persuading courts of their innocence, continue to support their efforts. Let no stone be unturned, no piece of evidence be ignored, no testimony muzzled that would exonerate the unjustly accused and convicted.

For those who face daily the drudgery and danger of prison life, we ask for renewed courage and your safekeeping. Help them to know that they are not alone, but that even in the shadows of lengthy or life sentences your grace is sufficient. For those who face the possibility of the imposition of death, may they know—even to the very end—your presence with them.

O God, by whose grace all of us have been forgiven of our sins and restored to the full measure of your acceptance of us, look with favor upon all who been have lifted up in this prayer. Grant as well to us who await the release of all prisoners the grace to welcome them back into our homes and communities, the resourcefulness to provide meaningful work and opportunities for self-betterment, and access to all of the joys, benefits, and challenges of our society.

Amen.

SAMUEL K. ROBERTS is the Anne Borden and E. Hervey Evans Professor of Theology and Ethics at Union Theological Seminary-Presbyterian School of Christian Education in Richmond, Virginia. Alongside his service as a pastor and theological educator for over thirty-five years, a life-long interest in the plight of the imprisoned was kindled in 1967 when, as a seminary intern at Union Theological Seminary in New York City, he conducted services at the Bronx and Brooklyn Houses of Detention. He is currently involved in a Richmond local church's outreach to mentor sons of men who are currently in prison.

<hr />

For the Word Keepers

O God, whose Word calls the worlds into being,

whose Word is announced by prophets and apostles,
whose Word of truth and grace has been made flesh in
Jesus Christ,

we praise thee for words and language, sentences and punctuation marks, paragraphs and pages. We thank thee for the power of words to reveal and for all language that evokes, provokes, and invokes. We praise thee for the awesome mysteries of speaking and of hearing, of writing, and of reading.

We pray, this day, for all who are servants of thy Word and stewards of our human words. And in particular we remember before you journalists and columnists, broadcasters and reporters, poets and novelists.

Fill these, Holy One, with a love of language and of life, a reverence for the power of words spoken and written, and a longing for the truth that heals the broken heart and mends the torn world.

O God, who has so ordered the human body as to give us two ears but one mouth, help us who speak and write to listen and to hear. Help us to listen with both our ears, one turned and tuned to the many-voiced world, another harkening and heeding our own true and particular voice.

Grant unto the word warriors powers of discernment and resistance: a capacity to discern and resist the distorting and distracting voices of vain ambition, of fear, of market and profit, of ease and torpor. In a society where events are spun, where perception trumps reality, and simple story lines are preferred to truth's complexity, we praise thee, O God, for all your faithful witnesses, those steady in their pursuit of the truth.

For journalists and columnists whose view behind life's various curtains puts them so often in a front row seat for cynicism, be a balm of hope and healing.

For poets and novelists who wonder if any in this blinkered, distracted age have eyes to see and ears to hear, be a word of encouragement and perseverance.

For broadcasters and reporters who risk themselves visible, grant courage to picture things aright.

For readers . . . thank you, good Lord! For listeners . . . bless your holy name! For all who await and seek your

Word in the midst of our many words . . . praise you! And when all the words run out, then still, Praise to You!

ANTHONY ROBINSON, an ordained minister in the United Church of Christ, is a columnist for the *Seattle Post-Intelligencer* newspaper. He is also the author of nine books, including *Transforming Congregational Culture* (2003) and *Common Grace: On Being a Person and Related Spiritual Matters* (2006).

For Those in Deep Water

Ancient of Days, God beyond all names of God, God above and below denominations, and Spirit of life and hope, draw near with your powerful energy and hear our prayer.

We are a people too well acquainted with danger, not secure in adventures or ready for risks. When we get afraid and want to turn back and forsake you, take us by the hand and touch our fear. Make us more afraid of fear than we are afraid. And grant us peace. Calm us "up."

Let terror cease, first in our hearts, then in our lands. Help us refuse our politicians' use of fear to promote themselves.

For risks not taken, for fears that paralyze us, for living shallow when the times are deep, for forgetting how much you love us, Mighty Seaworthy God, forgive us.

Grant us that rare kind of courage that Jesus knew and showed.

Let us be eager for the deep water, more afraid of silence than we are of speech, more afraid of risks refused than risks taken. Teach us to be chaos tolerant. And let our witness keep another from drowning. In the name of Spirited people everywhere, who plumb the depths so that we would know the way, we pray.

For the late shift at the nursing home, the young man about to become a suicide bomber, the migrant worker whose pay is delayed, the tired mother who still has to find the shoes before she can put her children to bed, the father who knows the car is failing but can't bear to tell its truth to a worried family, the son whose report card is going to be bad, the daughter whose soccer game is terrible and whose parents can't take the news — for all people who live in disturbed and deep water, for their fatigue and their persistence through it, we pray.

We ask for courage, for patience, for trust, for the refusal to substitute addictive calms for the real thing.

Bless all who struggle in small and large ways.

Bless our nation's leaders and politicians that they may find a way to stand tall in short times.

Bless the deep water in which we live that it be fruitful of our faith, courage, and your abundant grace.

Let terror cease and calm prevail, for all.

Amen.

DONNA SCHAPER is senior minister at Judson Memorial Church in New York City. A minister and writer in the United Church of Christ, she has also served as conference minister. She is active in the New Sanctuary Movement. Her most recent books are *Living Well While Doing Good* (2007) and *Grass Roots Gardening* (2007).

⌒⌒⌒

For Medical Professionals

God, Our Healer,

Help me heal this precious child, who lies so helpless before me. Let me be your instrument in this hour of need.

Microseconds are ticking away, marking what's left of this infant girl's will to live. Despite her six days of diarrhea, dehydration, fever, worsened by home remedies from the Ozark hills from hardscrabble parents trying to avoid doctor's bills they can't afford.

"Is it too late?" I'm afraid to ask in the emergency treatment room of the children's hospital, where I am an inexperienced intern, pretending that this thin, feverish tike can recover, can overcome the odds, with the help of modern medicine.

With all the fluids and glucose ready to go in suspended sterile flasks, all that I need to do is to find and thread my needle into a single lifesaving scalp vein of the tiny infant, who is in a state of near shock. In nearby treatment rooms I hear frantic bustling of all the other on-duty senior staff, doctors and nurses, completely absorbed in critical care of children from an auto accident.

That leaves the three of us, alone together in our cramped treatment room, overheated with the ceiling's surgical light bearing down on us: one student nurse, the infant, and me. Already perspiring from our aseptic gowns, we have only seconds to exchange glances as the baby is restrained from moving her head, as the needle tries to find a precious collapsing scalp vein. I wish I were more dexterous. I hold my breath as I try and miss the first available vein, leaving a nasty dark purple hematoma from the damage I inflicted. I glance up at the nurse, our breathing now synchronous, with our sense of urgency and desperation to get the fluids into the next collapsed vein.

I must pause, try to relax, and be calm. Looking up at my nurse companion, I recognize a country girl, from the same Ozark hill country, blue-eyed and blonde under her starched cap, wrapped in the oversized surgical gown. Her gaze is anxious, almost pleading, her forehead perspiring like mine. Her feminine but strong hands grasp the infant's head firmly, and she whispers to soothe the frightened, whimpering child.

Our eyes meet before I bend again over my end of the treatment table, our heads as close as movie lovers over cocktails, but this is no movie, especially for the frail life between us. "This could be my little sister back home," the nurse is thinking. "No wonder country folk don't trust city interns like you. . . . You don't know, don't understand, how hard Ozark life is . . . struggling to make ends meet where I grew up, fighting against hard times, poor soil, hunger, fear, and despair.

"Few of us in nursing ever go back home; it's too depressing."

Does she know, my treatment-table-forehead-to-forehead companion, how hard I am praying for skill, beyond my limits?

"Just this once, dear Lord, please guide me. Please steady this next slim vein. Don't let it buckle or bend, don't let me puncture it, please, before the fluids can trickle and flow, true and free, right to the thirsty tissues that need it so badly, the glucose, the precious salts, the oxygen pumping from her tiny brave Ozark heart."

It is in moments like this that we know how precious is the life You give us and acknowledge that, in life and in death, we belong to You.

Amen.

STAN SCHUMAN, MD, is a retired physician-epidemiologist with a career in teaching, research, and medical writing. Poetry has been his avocation since 1988. His roots are in East European Judaism. He is married to Joanna, a devout Episcopalian, and they have eight children and seventeen grandchildren.

⚭

For Gifts of Spirit for Doing Justice

Upon us, too, Lord, you promised to pour out your
  Spirit.

Come then, Holy Spirit, empower us to seek justice for
  the poor, the captive, the blind, and the oppressed
  of earth.

Deliver us from contentment with wealth that leaves
the poor to their own devices, the rich to get richer
yet, and the poor poorer still.

Stir us to construction of measures for restoring the
humanity of lawbreakers, lest we confuse construction of prisons with criminal justice.

Open the eyes of the powerful to see children who die
this day from starvation. Remind us that they are as
precious to you as are our own children to us, and
hasten the day when we no longer need forgiveness
for our stinginess.

Liberating Spirit, free us from idols that oppress
in the names of prosperity, national pride,
and privilege. Lead us not into the temptations
of comfort.

Deliver us from the evils of disdain for our neighbors.
Free us for reverence toward the things that matter.
Most of all, bless us with the perfect freedom of
worshiping you.

You know, Lord, that we too are poor, captive, blind,
and oppressed. We dare to claim the ministry of
Jesus as ministry to ourselves.

You have promised that those who ask will receive
from you your Spirit.

So come, Holy Spirit.

We ask it in company with all who pray with us this
day, in the name and in the promises of Jesus.

Amen.

DONALD W. SHRIVER JR., an ordained Presbyterian minister, served as a local pastor and university minister in North Carolina before becoming president of Union Theological Seminary in New York City, where he was also professor of Christian Ethics, 1975–96. He is author of some thirteen books and lives with his wife, Peggy, in New York City. His most recent book is *Honest Patriots: Loving a Country Enough to Remember Its Misdeeds* (2005).

For Business Leaders in a Global Era

We pray, O Lord, for those called to economic leadership in globalizing times. They have become the coordinators of new systems of finance, production, and exchange that are changing the face of the earth and the lives of multitudes.

They are the managers of the wealth of nations and the stewards of those technologies that are fateful for the well-being of the poor and of the ecological order. Through wondrous methods of extraction, manufacture, transportation, communication, and marketing, they have created a plenty for many that history has not heretofore seen. Their methods of organization break down old walls between nations and form bonds of interdependence between peoples who were once enemies or strangers. Their efficiencies generate job possibilities that draw millions from lives of subsistent drudgery into new, hopeful middle classes, as the cities of the world generate new industries.

We are thankful, O Lord, for those who lead the modern business corporations with integrity.

We pray also for those who have succumbed to the temptations of this occupation.

Some are tempted to forget that their calling is from You and that all they do is to be done under your watchful eye, according to your righteous laws, in concert with your holy purposes. Help them renew their sense of calling with a deepened profession of faith in your providence, and with the exercise of professional integrity in all dealings.

Some are tempted to confuse the legal duty to provide quality goods and services at a fair price with a selfish drive to maximize personal gain, ignoring the needs of others. Help them to see only just gain as due reward for creating wealth for the wider commonwealth, and to see employees, wholesalers, customers, and those left out as potential partners.

Some are tempted to see the laws of economics as the sovereign forces in human interaction and treat them alone as the mandatory calculations for all aspects of social life. Help them to see the dependence of economic development on a viable civil society that offers access to a nurturing faith, educational opportunity, a just legal system, and medical care.

Some are tempted by global competition to ignore the poor, exploit workers, squeeze suppliers, pollute the earth, or subcontract to those who do while pretending purity of intent. Help them to adopt practices that respect human rights and that cultivate abilities and trustworthiness, for all are made in your image.

We pray, O Lord, that these leaders not be led into such temptations. And if any have been, forgive the repentant hearts and set them on the path to fulfill their renewed calling.

And finally, dear God, we pray for those critics who see no possibility of a divine calling in the conduct of business, seeing only greed, materialism, and consumerism. Teach them that no sphere of human activity is beyond your care, and guide them as they work with those left out to learn the skills, habits, and commitments that would make them able to be creative participants and contributors to a flourishing and inclusive global society.

Amen.

MAX STACKHOUSE, a minister in the United Church of Christ, has taught Christian social ethics in several leading seminaries in the United States and in Asia and is the author or editor of twelve books, including a cross-cultural study of human rights and a series on God and Globalization, including the recent *Globalization and Grace*. He also prepared a "lost" early book of Walter Rauschenbusch's for publication and is an expert on the social gospel period.

For Peace Seekers

Lean close, O Holy God!
Lean close and hear the weeping hearts
of your people who seek peace!

The map of your world is dark with death!
Your earth is saturated with the blood of your
   children!
The innocents cry for help and are answered
   with silence.
War and terror stalk us! Fear is at every doorstep.
O God, your people are killing one another!
Sometimes in your name!
We who seek peace raise our voices to sing
and are drowned out by explosive obscenities
   of hatred.
We walk the path of peace and are stopped by a
   world on fire with war.
We are taunted by sounds of derision . . .
and sometimes in your name!

O God, bless the peace seekers! O God, give us
   your hand!
Give us patience, O God, when our faith falters.
Give us stamina to stand up and walk in your peace!

Give us tenderheartedness for those who think war
    is the answer.
Give the world the eyes to see the absurdity
    of killing!
Soften the hearts of all nations, O Holy One,
and have mercy upon us all!
Come, O Holy God, come, and save your world!

Pull your church into its pulpits to preach your
    word of peace!
Pull your people onto rooftops to sing their song
    of peace!
Give us new voices, O God!
Give us new songs!
Give us new hearts for one another, for all the
    one anothers!!
Give us new hope!
Give us new life!
O God, send angels!
Send miracles!
Send love!
Send peace!

In the name of Jesus,
whose birth was surrounded by the angels' song
    of peace, goodwill,
whose life was a covenant of peace and love,
whose death and resurrection were the ultimate
    word of your grace!
We give you thanks, O God, for your neverending
    gift of Life!
Amen.

ANN WEEMS, an elder in the Presbyterian Church (U.S.A.), is a
poet, speaker, liturgist, workshop leader, and author of numerous
books.

For Disciples

Lord Jesus,

Why did you so recklessly put your treasure in such a frail, earthen vessel? Why did you give over your kingdom and its work to a servant as unworthy as I? What were you thinking when you entrusted a coward like me with the keys to your kingdom, with the power to bind and to loose? Having erred in your calling of Judas, why compound your mistake by calling me to be your disciple?

I thought I was unselfish until I met you. I knew not the depth of my deceit until you told me. Before I was summoned, I slept well. My life was easier when I lived it for myself.

Therefore, in my weakness, in my ineptitude to give you the fidelity you deserve, I am bold to pray for all those who will be unable to see your great love because of my poor discipleship:

I pray for all those whom you have made my brothers and sisters, but whom I still regard as strangers.

I pray for all those whom I pass by on the other side, failing to notice their need, failing to stop and do for them what I can.

I pray for those who don't have enough to eat while I and my family have too much.

I pray for those whom my nation has taught me to despise as enemies when you gave your life for them as your friends.

I pray for all those whom I should have forgiven in obedience to your command, but against whom I found it safer to keep score.

I pray for all those who have suffered injustice twice, once by the injustice committed against them and again by my failure to speak up for them and to stand beside them.

I pray for all those who have almost lost faith in your ability to transform lives because they tire of waiting for me to at last do the right thing.

Lord Jesus, even as you miraculously made bread for the hungry multitudes and turned water into wine, could you please work just one more wonder? Make me, your mistake of judgment, into your faithful, obedient disciple, testimony to your power to commandeer a life and make it fit for your kingdom. I have faith that you can do even this.
Amen.

WILLIAM H. WILLIMON is the author of many influential books on the church and its ministry. He is former dean of the chapel at Duke University and bishop of the United Methodist Church, Birmingham, Alabama.

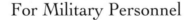

For Military Personnel

God, by all names recognized by peoples of our world,
to those who dedicate their lives to the protection of
their fellow citizens
by serving in the military of their countries,
grant them the wisdom to serve but not be subservient
to unlawful decisions of civilian administrations.

May their concern for the defense of their country
guide them in the determination of lawful and
unlawful orders

and grant them the wisdom and courage to protect,
    not torture.
May their acts of physical courage be matched by
    acts of conscience.

May young men and women be offered opportunities
    for education
so they do not feel that military service is their only
    opportunity for advancement
in societies that glorify militarism
and put peacemakers on criminal lists.

May those who join the military and then refuse
    to kill others
be understood by their superiors
and allowed to end their military service honorably,
not in a jail cell.

May those in command have the strength to resist
    unlawful orders;
to protect civilians and abide by the original Geneva
    Conventions;
to reject torture for those in their custody
and to tell the truth, no matter what the consequences.

May those in command care for those under their
    command;
acknowledge the costs of war on emotions and
    conscience,
of not only those in the military, but family members
    at home.
May those in the military work for peace and not
    violence.

May they be strong against retaliation and retribution.
May they be understanding when their colleagues
    and friends

disagree with their act of conscience and turn against
    them.
May they know that standing for the greater
    good inevitably
results in personal sacrifice and sometimes even
    imprisonment.
May they be strong knowing their consciences
    are clean.

MARY A. (ANN) WRIGHT served for twenty-nine years in the army
and army reserves, shifting to the reserves upon entering the foreign
service. She served primarily in special operations units and attained
the rank of colonel. Her foreign service assignments included postings
in Micronesia, Afghanistan, Sierra Leone, Somalia, and Uzbekistan.
She resigned from the U.S. Foreign Service in protest at the outset of
the second Iraq war while serving as deputy chief of mission in Mongo-
lia, and has since spoken and written widely on U.S. foreign policy.

7

PRAYERS FOR THE EARTH

For Creation

This prayer was adapted by Rita Nakashima Brock from the Immolatio and Post-Sanctus of the Gallican Eucharist Rite of the eighth century. The original text can be found in *Prayers of the Eucharist: Early and Reformed* (3rd ed., eds. R. C. D. Jasper and C. J. Cuming [Collegeville, MN: Liturgical Press, 1990], 148–49). The editors write, "The name 'Gallican' strictly applies to the rite used in France until its supersession by the Roman rite completed by Charlemagne c. 800; but it is used in a wider sense to include . . . a family of non-Roman Latin rites. All these rites tend to show more traces of Eastern influence than does the native Roman rite. . . . Some of the prayers are clearly of great antiquity, predating the Roman canon in its historic form" (147).

Eternal God, You gave wonderful forms to the amazed
　　elements:
the tender world blushed at the fires of the sun,
and the sleeping seas wondered at the tug of the moon.

Lest no inhabitant should adorn all this
and the sun's orb shine on emptiness,
you made from clay two more excellent
    likenesses,
which a holy fire quickened within
and a lively spirit brought to life throughout their
    idle parts.
We may not look, O God, fully into the inner
    mysteries.
To you alone is known the full majesty of your work.

What there is in us:
the blood held in the veins that washes the flexing
    limbs,
the loose bodies that are held together by tightening
    nerves,
and the straight bones that gain strength from the
    organs within.

Whence comes so great a bounty to humble
    humanity
that we should be formed in the likeness of you and
    your Child,
that an earthly thing should be eternal?
Yet we have often abandoned the care of your blessed
    majesty in creation
and mourn the ways we have betrayed your beautiful
    world.

But your manifold goodness and inestimable majesty
    sent the saving Wisdom from heaven,
that Word should be made flesh by taking a human
    body,
that your Savior should care for that which we might
    have lost,
and that your Spirit healed our ancient wounds.

Therefore all the angels,
with the manifold multitude of the saints praise you.
They proclaim your magnificence,
made in the starry realms and descended to earth.
We lift our voices in praise to welcome what was
    revealed to us by a gift,
not only to be known but also to be imitated
and, in living its truth, to be made whole again.
Amen.

RITA NAKASHIMA BROCK is codirector of Faith Voices for the Common Good, senior editor in religion for The New Press, and a visiting scholar at Starr King School for the Ministry in Berkeley, California. She is author of several award-winning books and writes on ethics for *Politics* and on the lectionary for *Disciples World*. Her latest book is *Saving Paradise: How Christianity Traded Love of This World for Crucifixion and Empire.*

❦

For the Beauty of Creation

Almighty and everlasting God,
    You created the world as a bountiful garden, bringing life to every creature that moves and breathes. We thank thee for the vitality, beauty, and fruit of your creation. We pray that our roots would grow deep in the rich soil of your Word. Water us daily with the subterranean river of life. From seed to sapling, may we grow to be sturdy oaks of righteousness, radiating light in dark places. With time may the girth of our trunks be hearty and sap thick in protection against those who destroy. May our branches reach out to the high heavens, and our falling leaves drift to lands far and wide for the healing of the nations.
    Rejoice, O ye Earth, rejoice! We wait and watch with the eyes of ravens and the patience of ancient trees for that day when the trumpet shall sound and the trees of the

fields shall clap their hands. Let thy Spirit go forth quickly, that it may renew the face of the earth.

Friends on earth and friends above, let's burst forth God's peace and love; through Jesus Christ our Lord. Amen.

PETER HELTZEL teaches theology at New York Theological Seminary in New York. A member of the Christian Church/Disciples of Christ, he is a native of Mississippi and active in evangelical social justice movements. His book *Jesus and Justice* is forthcoming in 2008.

For the Broken Earth

We believe it is your good earth, O God, and our celebration of your world is tempered by our recognition of the pollution that surrounds us, most of which is our own creation. The water is full of chemicals, the air is heavy with pollution, the rain is killing the trees, and we are scared. We are tampering with the grand scheme of things in ways that both bless us and contaminate us and the earth; its air, sea, and land are stretched to the breaking point.

Give us courage to speak out in moments such as this, but open our own eyes to see how we are the problem in ways large and small—we and the processing plants that are so destructive. We want justice, until it inconveniences us. We whine about the strip mines, but we patronize the strip malls. We are all accomplices in the rush to rob the earth.

So forgive us this day our daily pollutions, and give us strength to change our ways. Let us speak out to the powerful, who can change policies even as we examine our own lives and lifestyles. Help us to change the little habits that seem innocent until multiplied by six billion. With the psalmist let us lift up our eyes to the hills, Your hills and mountains, O God, and seek your help, for our going out and coming in, from this day forth and even forever more. Amen.

BILL LEONARD is dean of Wake Forest Divinity School. He has held teaching posts at Southern Baptist Theological Seminary, Samford University, and Seinan Gakuin University (Fukuoka, Japan). He is the author or editor of fifteen books, including his most recent book *Baptists in America* (2005).

To Overcome Our Fear of Chaotic Abundance

Sweet Lord of Creation,

You made a beautiful world, rich and decadent in its diversity. It is so lush and full of variety and possibility that it overwhelms us with its rich chaos. We find ourselves yearning to be part of this rich abundance, and yet we fear being lost in its chaotic glory. So we try and press it into an order we can understand. Unfortunately that order is unable to see the creation through your eyes.

In simplifying creation so that it makes sense in our finite minds, we try to tame the abundance by removing what we think is unnecessary or wasteful. We forget that what in our eyes is wasteful or unnecessary may be in your eyes precious and indispensable. You made the creation purposefully in its wasteful, resourceful abundance and called it good. You grieve when any species or natural marvel becomes extinct.

Forgive us the weakness that comes with our finiteness. Give us the faith in you and your purpose that allows us to overcome our fear of the chaotic abundance of your creation. Reopen our eyes and our hearts to what we saw as waste to see it anew with your eyes. Help us to see the rich wonderful delight with which you imbued the very things and people whom we decided did not fit in our simple patterns of order and dismissed as irrelevant.

We know your enriching grace can give us the faith to readdress all the things and people our fear silences and dismisses. Rather than breaking and re-forming your creation to fit our orders, may we experience even our breaking as the re-forming of your wilder and wiser order. Then we can actually participate in the rich abundance of the world as you would wish us to. With your grace, we could even become advocates of that abundance. We could be champions of those we once victimized. We can become the stewards of creation you intended us to be. Bless us so that we can become a blessing.

In your holy name we pray,
Amen.

DAMAYANTHI NILES is a minister of Word and Sacrament in the Presbyterian Church (U.S.A.) and associate professor of constructive theology at Eden Theological Seminary. Her writing and research focus on constructive and contextual theology. She has taught courses in foundational theology, missiology, and postcolonial thought. Born in Sri Lanka, she has also served as a research associate of the Christianity in Asia Project at the Centre for Advanced Religious and Theological Studies at Cambridge University, United Kingdom.

For the Earth and Her Creatures

God of Majesty, Lord of Mercy, Spirit of Mystery,
your glory saturates the cosmos
    from the tiniest creature to the farthest flung
      universe.
Your light irradiates every atom,
    every living being within and under heaven.
Your wisdom echoes in each flower and tree,
    river and mountain, bird and beast.

Holy and Blessed One,
the grace of your creation is incomparable.
What we cannot fully fathom we yet bless you for,
    fulfilling the circle of communion for which you
        made us —
    forever receiving life in gratitude,
    forever blessing your endless gifts of love.

Great God of Truth,
we grieve for the wounds of your beautiful earth,
    wounds inflicted by our own carelessness,
        ignorance, and greed.
We mourn whole species of your magnificent crea-
    tures,
    whose extinction parallels our inordinate desire
        for goods,
    our insatiable appetite for overabundance.
We confess that we waste our powers on what holds
    little lasting value,
    neglecting and abusing the very gifts of nature
    that would refresh our souls and restore our sanity.
Your presence lies hidden deep within all you have made;
you infuse creation with your grace,
    making it transparent to your love and life-giving
        to our spirit.
Therefore keep us mindful that our care for the least
    of your creatures
    is a salve to your love in this world.
May we not refuse the priceless gift of your grace
    for the sake of lesser pleasures that dull the soul
    and impoverish the voiceless among us.

Merciful Lord, open our ears to the groaning
    of creation:
    glaciers melting into a rising sea,
    polar bears swimming to exhaustion in search of ice,

wetlands drying to parched cracks,
songbirds seeking ancient sanctuaries in vain,
coral reefs bleaching in polluted waters,
whales beaching themselves in despair.

Awaken us, Good Lord, to our responsibility
for this earth over which you made us stewards.
Give us your spirit of compassion for all you
have made,
your delight in the vast joy and beauty of nature.

Help us to know deeply the truth
of our interconnection with all creatures;
to acknowledge how we feed on common foods,
breathe the same air,
drink from the shared waters of this planet.

May we perceive how the limited store
of earth's elements
cycle round from age to age,
that we may commit to keep them clean and pure.
Thus may we honor our bodies,
cherishing the gift of health you graciously intend
and offering well-being to others for all generations
to come.

Teach us so to value our vocation as caretakers
of creation
that the earth and every thread of her living fabric
may, as you have promised,
come to share in the very freedom of the children
of God.

In the name of the One through and for whom
all things have been created,
and in whom all things hold together.
Amen.

MARJORIE J. THOMPSON is an ordained minister in the Presbyterian Church (U.S.A.). The author of two books, including the widely acclaimed *Soul Feast,* she serves as director of Pathways in Congregational Spirituality at Upper Room Ministries in Nashville, Tennessee. In this capacity she has for ten years guided the development of Companions in Christ, a small-group resource series in spiritual formation that now includes versions for children and youth. Marjorie delights in the wonders of creation and holds an abiding concern for ecological responsibility.

8

PRAYERS FOR REPENTANCE AND TRANSFORMATION

To Claim God's Vision of a New Earth

O God, creator of the universe, master builder and architect of all things possible. Let me claim your vision of a new heaven and a new earth.

In your vision, those who build houses will dwell in them. Those who plant vineyards will eat their fruit. No longer will they build houses and others live in them, or plant and others eat, says the prophet Isaiah (Isa. 65:21–22)

But we live in a society in which those who care for children struggle to afford child care.

Those who provide home health care for seniors have no health care for themselves.

Those who clean rooms in resort hotels can't afford to stay in a hotel.

Day laborers who help build homes cannot live in them.

And the children of those who plant and harvest our food go hungry.

Please forgive my collusion with a twisted world that devalues work and hurts your people. I participate and sometimes benefit from this devaluing of work. Forgive me. Forgive me when my search for cheap deals encourages companies to cheat workers. Forgive me when I forget to recognize that my food comes from workers' hands. Forgive me when I follow the market's standards instead of your standards in paying people.

Lead me to a new heaven and a new earth. Remove my desire for more worldly goods in the midst of such poverty. Inflame my passion for justice. Create in me a vision of society in which those who build live and those who plant eat.

Amen.

KIM BOBO is the executive director of Interfaith Worker Justice, an organization based in Chicago that provides resources for workers and workers' organizations across the United States. Her positive spirit helps sustain labor efforts that are sometimes besieged.

For Courage

It's not as if we don't know, dear God. You have told us simply and clearly that what you want and require from us is justice and kindness, and that you invite us to walk humbly with you. You have shown us in the life of your Son, our Lord Jesus Christ, that in your kingdom the hungry are fed, the homeless sheltered, the captives set free, the excluded included. And as he died on a cross, executed by the state for challenging authority, confronting convention, extending love across all the barriers and boundaries that provided his people and their oppressors with stability and security, you have demonstrated that to follow him means summoning courage to challenge, confront, and extend love as he did.

We pray for that courage. We confess that we do not always have it or want it. We confess that, like people in one of his best stories, we walk by on the other side of the road, without seeing, feeling, or stopping to acknowledge the needs of those who are wounded by the world's violence, neglect, prejudice, and ignorance. We confess that we are not only too preoccupied to stop and kneel by the side of the wounded but afraid of where it might lead us and what it might require us to do. So we pray for courage.

We pray for your church, grateful for those occasions when it spoke and acted in the world as he did: grateful for the courage of those who confronted authority and paid the price, marching, demonstrating, remonstrating, speaking, writing letters, telephoning politicians, representing your holy calling to do justice and love kindness. We pray for your church, sometimes struggling for its life against persecution, sometimes against indifference: fill it with your Spirit to be the body of your son, willing to forsake its own survival and safety in order to serve you and your kingdom.

And, dear God, do remind us that death did not defeat him, could not hold him: that your dearest promise is that there is no power in this world capable of defeating the power of your love. Do remind us, in the midst of our doubts and discouragements, that your kingdom is coming, that love overcomes evil and death.

All this we pray in the name of our crucified and risen Lord Jesus Christ.

Amen.

JOHN BUCHANAN has been pastor of the Fourth Presbyterian Church of Chicago since 1985. He has held numerous other leadership positions in the Presbyterian Church (U.S.A.) including serving as Moderator of the 208th General Assembly. In addition to his ministry in the church he serves as the editor/publisher of the *Christian Century*.

For Mutual Forgiveness

Most gracious God,

You care about all of us, all human beings, and everything else as well, and as we bring ourselves consciously into your presence, we would expand our caring as well. But as we do so, our hearts grow heavy with the awareness of all the harm that we human beings, and especially we Americans, are doing to one another and to our world. We can hardly imagine the suffering that is yours as you share in the suffering of the world.

We rejoice that life is not all suffering. Indeed, for many of us the lines have fallen in pleasant places. We are surrounded by people we love and have much more than the necessities of life. The beauty of the world never ceases to astound us. Of course, even we privileged ones know sorrow and disappointment, sickness, and the death of loved ones. We, too, regret our failures and confess our sins. We know that even now, day by day, we participate in and contribute to a society that imposes its will on others by force of arms and economic power, and that devastates the earth, consuming far more than our share of its resources. But we live joyfully in the consciousness of your acceptance and forgiveness.

We do not want to presume on your love and to continue unreflectively to harm our neighbors and our fellow creatures or to rob the future. We would end our national bullying of others and our preoccupation with sustaining our "way of life" at their expense. Help us to find another way to live with joy while sharing the earth's resources and living in a sustainable way.

Help us to resist those cultural and social trends that move us as a people ever more deeply into the worship of mammon. Help us to resist our national goal of "full spectrum dominance." Help us to resist the sort of secularization that undercuts the ideals of personal discipline and unselfish service. Help us to resist the deceptions and distortions by which our government, our media, and even our universities increase support for destructive actions.

We thank you that you not only strengthen our resistance but also work in transforming ways throughout our world. Our hope is in you: in the everyday miracles you are constantly working everywhere; in the wonderful miracles you work in us, widening our horizons and sensitizing our hearts; and in the occasional miracles you manage to work in the ongoing course of history, when you guide leaders to end conflicts between races or nations. Use us, if it be your will, in bringing reason to an irrational world and life to a dying one.

We pray in the name of one who gave his life in the cause of mutual forgiveness, of justice, and of a peace that passes understanding: Jesus Christ, our Lord.

Amen.

JOHN COBB was born in Japan to Methodist missionary parents and became a Methodist minister, though one called to integrate scientific, philosophical, and theological thought in process theology. His work has included pastoral theology and, in partnership with economist Herman Daly, an ecologically far-sighted revisioning of economic growth. He recently edited *Progressive Christians Speak* (2000; reprinted 2003).

For a Spiritual Awakening

It's so easy to get lost in our world today, O God. Lost in the grim realities of poverty and war. Lost in the grip of disasters both natural and human made. Lost in the lust for power or wealth masquerading as answers to our world's problems.

Lost in our own inflated egos — or our imperviousness to the world around us. We confess how often we allow our lives to be overwhelmed by that which we see around us, or by our own thoughts and motives and desires. And then when we wander, both individually and when we are together as your people, we wonder where you have gone.

In this lost and broken world you so love, O God, send us anew your guiding Spirit. Open our eyes to your presence. Change our hearts, challenge our minds, and deepen our spirits, so that we may see and embrace the world's pain and hope even as you have embraced the world. Break into our confusion. Silence in us our own selfish desires. Awaken us to your service, that with boldness, courage, and compassion we might turn ourselves to the world, seeking justice, sparking revival, igniting a movement for renewal of our communities and our world.

Shape our witness, O God, that at every point, in every life, with every group, in every nation, the love of Christ can break through and flow, making all things new.

Amen.

THE REV. WESLEY GRANBERG-MICHAELSON was installed as general secretary of the Reformed Church in America at its 1994 General Synod. Granberg-Michaelson served for six years on the staff of the World Council of Churches (WCC) in Geneva, Switzerland (1988–1994). He has also served as managing editor for *Sojourners* magazine and as president of the New Creation Institute in Missoula, Montana, working on issues of Christian responsibility for the environment as well as the church's role in healing and health. He is the author of three books, most recently *Leadership from Inside Out* (2004).

ᗢᗣ

For a Nation's Change of Heart

O God,

We American Christians pray, "Your kingdom come, your will be done on *earth* as in heaven," but I wonder if we recognize the potential consequences when we pray those words.

> *Your kingdom come* might mean that we who turn luxuries into necessities would only have necessities.
> *Your kingdom come* might mean that we who live to eat would only eat to live.
> *Your kingdom come* might mean that we who have such great hopes would moderate our hopes in order that others might have hope.

Jesus pictured graphically for us what kingdom character requires. Those invited into the kingdom are the ones who feed the hungry, give drink to the thirsty, clothe the naked, take strangers into their homes—in short, the ones who meet human need wherever or in whatever form they find it without even thinking about it.

O God of mercy, we Americans like to think that we are a righteous people, a good and godly people, but America's righteousness today seems far removed from kingdom righteousness: One-fifth of American citizens take in half of all household income whereas one-tenth pull in just a little less than forty percent. One percent lay claim to just under twenty percent, with more than one hundred million people (33 percent) on the bottom. Whereas in 1980 the average CEO got forty-two times the pay of the average worker, in 2004 the CEO "merited" 358 times as much. And tax rates on the superwealthy fell from 91 percent in the 1950s to 35 percent today; corporate rates, from 35 percent in 1945 to 10 percent today.

When one looks at how these statistics translate into people, we see that 13 percent of Americans, mostly single-parent families, live in poverty; and 20 percent of America's children live in poverty. There are more than 750,000 homeless Americans, and 47,000,000 have no health insurance.

O God of infinite compassion, Jesus told for us the parable of the Rich Man and a poor beggar named Lazarus. On earth the rich man had it all. Dressed in resplendent clothes, he enjoyed life every day. He scarcely noticed the poor beggar deposited daily at his doorstep, hoping against hope that a few crumbs might fall his way from the table of the rich man. Dogs licked his wounds. Then came heaven's reversal. When both died, the poor man found himself in the bosom of Abraham, the rich man in a place of torment, repenting—but too late! He couldn't even arrange a wake-up call for the family he left behind except the message that he had had—Moses and the prophets.

How do we measure up, Lord? How do we measure up? Some surveys show we Americans are generous as individuals. Most Americans give in moments of crisis—

for the tsunami in the Indian Ocean basin;
for earthquakes in Pakistan and Turkey;
for hurricane Katrina;
to churches, schools, hospitals, institutions, and pro-
    grams of care, beggars, and panhandlers.

But are we generous as a *nation*? Here we present a very different picture, Lord. Possessed of incredible wealth, we fall near the bottom of the developed nations in percentage of our gross national product given to aid underdeveloped nations. And our giving usually comes with strings attached.

Over against such a pitiful outlay for building up, America has already spent more than $600 billion in the "War on Terrorism," the greater part of it in an, at best, highly questionable effort at establishing "democracy" in Iraq. We have become so concerned about America's security that we now "preempt" our enemies and destabilize the security of the rest of the world!

I pray for the one thing I can think will matter here—a change of heart for a whole nation. A change of heart, *metanoia*, repentance, is the heart of the matter. And only you, O God of infinite love, can change this nation's heart.

In your infinite love, cast out the fear that stands in the
way of change to a more equitable and caring society in America.
In your unfailing mercy, replace our *hubris* with
humility.
In your unlimited compassion, sensitize and conscien-
tize and tenderize us to see the world through
your eyes.
In your great wisdom, enable us to elect leaders who
know and live your love and compassion for all.
In your eternal hopefulness, grant us a vision of your
kingdom come and your will done on earth as in
heaven.

We pray in the name of the one who taught us to dare to
say, "Your kingdom come, your will be done on earth, as it
is in heaven."
Amen and Amen!

E. GLENN HINSON is professor emeritus of spirituality and John F.
Loftis Professor of Church History at Baptist Theological Seminary at
Richmond. In retirement he teaches at Baptist Seminary of Kentucky,
Louisville Presbyterian Theological Seminary, and Bellarmine Univer-
sity. An ordained Baptist minister, he has served on the Faith and
Order Commissions of the World Council of Churches and National
Council of Churches. He has written or edited twenty-seven books and
more than twelve hundred articles and book reviews.

Prophetic Witness: A Prayer
of Remembrance and Hope

Loving God of righteousness, of mercy,
and of possibility:
We bless you for lovingly creating us to be in
community, to be in relation.

Thank you for the beauties of creation, of life,
    of our very being.
You call us to do justice and to be in relationships
    of loving-kindness
with our neighbor, our community, our country,
    our universe, and ourselves.
We confess our failures to love our neighbors,
    ourselves, and you!

We fail to love our neighbors as poverty abounds
    domestically and globally.
We demonize the poor, in fear of lack and disregard.
Forgive us for allowing thousands to die and be
    displaced midst Katrina, storms, and drought.
We confess the lack of empathy shown by our
    governments and by our churches.
Help the spirits of the dead from war, strife,
    and madness rest in your loving presence.
Help us to love survivors concretely with pastoral
    care, resources, and spiritual encouragement.
    Our human callousness is an abomination that
    cries to you for peace.
Forgive us for our denial and disrespect;
for using categories of gender, age, race, sexual
    orientation, and socioeconomics to punish.
Kyrie, eléison, Christe eléison, Kyrie eléison.

We confess our failure to love our children well.
We assume preparation for parenthood,
but fail to acknowledge our pathologies and character
    defects.
We perpetrate our shortcomings on our children,
    within our families, and within our society.
We confess our inadequacies in disciplining our youth.
    We have allowed ideologies like "No Child Left
    Behind"

to cripple our marginalized children as they are forced
   to study for "The Test"
and are not taught to know their histories and to think
   critically.
We have not valued them as your children —
   our children.
Objectified and minimized, our children, who have
   been taught
not to love themselves or others, have become
   self-fulfilling prophecies.
Our criminal justice system is bursting with adult
   children
whose problems began as emotional distress and
   mental illness.
Now, they murder, plunder, and rape.

We confess our failure to have a flexible society:
people who are shy, withdrawn, or deemed different
   are often harassed and ridiculed.
While such episodes occur daily,
we deny the cruelty of children and adults to others
until violence explodes at schools:
the 2007 Virginia Tech murders by Cho Seung-hui;
the 2006 siege and Amish schoolhouse murders
   by Charles Carl Roberts IV;
the 1999 Columbine massacre by Eric Harris and
   Dylan Klebold;
the 1966 Texas Tower sniper murders by Charles S.
   Whitman.
Just-seeking God, we know you grieve with us,
with all the families and friends of all who died
   senselessly
during these acts of terror.
Help us to better understand and compassionately
   help those
who suffer from mental and emotional disorders;

those who bully and are bullied;
those who gravitate toward subcultures of crime
and violence.
Help us help them before they commit horrible acts
of vengeance.

Merciful God:
Historically we have perpetrated and defended
violence by church and state,
where bloodshed and abuse have occurred in the
name of progress, messianism, ideology:
from the slavery of plantations and reservations,
the "Trail of Tears," Japanese internment camps,
and Chinese indentured rail workers
to Wounded Knee, Kent State, Jonestown, Ruby
Ridge, and Waco.
In the twenty-first century, help us to do justice at
all times,
to honor the humanity of everyone, to embrace difference,
and to transform our systems of family, church,
education, and government
to incarnate the social gospel of loving our neighbor.
Kyrie, eléison Christe, eléison, Kyrie, eléison.

THE REV. DR. CHERYL A. KIRK-DUGGAN is a professor of theology
and women's studies at Shaw University Divinity School, Raleigh,
North Carolina, and an ordained elder in the Christian Methodist Episcopal Church. She recently authored *Violence and Theology* (2006) and
edited *The Sky Is Crying: Racism, Classism, and Natural Disaster* (2006).

─────────────── ∞◯◯ ───────────────

That We May Not Be Distracted
by False Images

Gracious One, awaken us to the real suffering and real
hope that surround us each day. Remove the scales from

our eyes. In a culture distracted by false images of the good life—in a culture ruled by distorted desires and nameless fears—redirect our desire toward those things that make for peace and reconciliation. Redirect our attention from clueless celebrities and pandering politicians toward the everyday heroes in our midst who live out your gospel call against overwhelming odds. Ground us in truth and love. Remove our fear. In a winner-take-all culture, remind us that each person made in your image is as worthy of respect and as deserving of the good things of life as any other.

Grant us that most precious spiritual gift of ethical clarity, from which true repentance may yet flow. As we in our fool's paradise finally begin to recognize that we "grope like the blind along a wall . . . we wait for justice but there is none; for salvation, but it is far from us . . . for truth stumbles in the public square" (Isa. 59:10-11,14), let us also remember that your hand is not too short to save, nor your ear too dull to hear, if we would but turn toward ways of solidarity and inclusion.

Deliver us, dear God, from remaining illusions that this nation is specially anointed to be a beacon to other nations. Permit us to be realistic about the violence and oppression that represent the actual footprint of the United States in a suffering world. Deliver us from cheap grace, we pray, and from all idolatries of flag and altar. Teach us what faithful discipleship means—and what it may cost us—living in the heart of an empire marked by decadence and domination. Help us to love our country not for what it is now but for what it might yet be if we are willing to give up our idols, turn from our distractions, and walk humbly in your way.

Amen.

THE REV. PETER LAARMAN is executive director of Progressive Christians Uniting, a fast-growing ecumenical network of individuals and congregations headquartered in Los Angeles. Laarman served for ten years as senior minister of Judson Memorial Church in New York City prior to coming to California. He is the editor of a book of essays titled *Getting On Message: Challenging the Christian Right from the Heart of the Gospel* (2006).

⚬⚬⚬

To Know the Daring Spirit of God's Humility

O Lord Jesus, you did not grasp after equality with God as we so often delude ourselves into doing. We confess that in our overreaching we have lost our way, our core, and much of our humanity. Out of loneliness, guilt, and anxiety, we pray for the healing spirit of your humility through which you embodied God's love for us all — a healing spirit that embraces the least of us and extends to those we shun, judge, and condemn, even our enemies.

In humility you identified with the poor, the sick, the alien, the oppressed, and the exploited, those of our human family we often forget in our pursuit of personal gain and private privilege. With disregard for self, you confronted hypocrites, the self-absorbed, the abusers of power, and the addicts of prominence, inviting them, and so us, to risk changing for the sake of God's kingdom. For our benefit and example, you humbly and willingly paid the price of such love, and in your resurrection God confirmed its power.

Now we ask from our heart to yours, raise us and step out with us on the promise of your life. At our crossroad of humility or arrogance, hope or despair, courage or fear, trust or cynicism, enable us to choose the way you have composed in us as the deepest longing of our hearts.

> Enable us to work for justice without becoming arrogant or unjust, that the human family may flourish.
> Enable us to be courageous without being foolish or violent, that we may learn what love means.
> Enable us to grow in wisdom without trivializing the mystery of God's grace, that we may live in awe.

Enable us to trust God and live boldly without claiming certainty, that we may be truly free.

Enable us to resist stifling conformity and act creatively for the welfare of all, that we may find peace.

Enable in us a humility that takes God more seriously than we take ourselves, that hope may abide.

Grant us, then, glad hearts, tough minds, daring spirits, songs to sing in the night, joy in the morning, and abiding trust that the promises we step out on hold us tight and guide us North-Star-true. Guide us as deeds of compassion are done for the poor, the sick, the young and old, the whole human family, and this amazing earth you gave us to share and care for as home.

Help us discover again and again who we are: daughters and sons created in the image of God, beloved prodigals of your kingdom, and brothers and sisters in love with time to act like it.

We pray in your name and spirit.

Amen.

TED LODER served as pastor of the First United Methodist Church of Germantown in Philadelphia, Pennsylvania, for thirty-seven years. Under Loder's leadership the church became a Public Sanctuary Church; a founding church of the Covenant against Apartheid in South Africa; a Reconciling Congregation advocating for the rights of homosexual persons in opposition to national church policy; and sent delegations to and supports local missions in Guatemala, Haiti, and South Africa. He is also well known for his inspirational writings published in books such as *Guerillas of Grace* (originally published 1984; reprinted 2005).

☙❧

A Prayer for Civil Rights

Bishop Vashti Murphy McKenzie delivered this prayer at the Memphis Civil Rights Museum Freedom

Awards Banquet in late 2006, starting with a brief introduction.

The psalmist speaks across the centuries to remind us of a time when "kindness and truth shall meet; justice and peace shall kiss" (Ps. 85:11). The classic summary of what Yahweh asks in covenant with all humankind is what Dr. Martin Luther King Jr. calls the "*magna carta* of prophetic religion," where God asks of us only this: "to act justly, to love tenderly and to walk humbly with your God" (Mic. 6:8). These three mandates cannot be separated, according to Thomas H. Groome: "As people do justice with loving kindness, their faith as right relationship with God is realized." Let us pray.

Merciful God, who has been our dwelling place for many generations; we invoke your presence tonight to ask you to quicken our hearts that we may be swift to hear the cries of others from the pit of need. Enlarge our hearts to embrace with love the world larger than our own; help us to have special regard for and respond to the poor and weak, sick and frail, the very young and the very old, whether it is in Memphis or Darfur; the Mississippi Delta or Afghanistan; Haiti or Henderson County; Rwanda or Rhode Island.

Remind us once again of the brave dreams of freedom and justice that were born in the hearts of our ancestors; the dreams they were willing to live and die for; the battles they valiantly fought in the courthouse, the school yard, the classroom, and the streets. Grant us courage to continue to flesh out their dreams; grant us wisdom to reshape the strategy for this present age. O God, let us not be weary in well-doing as we confront the ancient enemies again: injustice, poverty, apathy, racism, and sexism. Behind them all stands an implacable evil

that stains the tapestry of the twenty-first century with the blood of the innocent and unsuspecting;

that rapes our communities with unprecedented violence, when school children choose death over life
in suicide attacks on classmates;
that shouts the sounds of wars and rumors of war daily.

If we fall, help us to rise again and put within us a faith and
hope that cannot be quenched. Inspire all harassed and
struggling souls of every race, nation, creed, and hue with
the assurance that all the forces of good are working for
them and are moving them on to peace, health, and holiness.

Shine your light in us in such a way that we see all
of humankind as brothers and sisters; shine your light
through us to bring a new vision of equality. Help us to see
that our freedom doesn't demand the enslavement of others; shine your light on us so that others can see that even
though we are marred and broken vessels, you still use us
as channels of your grace to bring mercy, joy, and peace
into the lives of our fellow pilgrims on this journey of life.
We seek the pure light of thy holiness so that we may find
our way in this world to do justly, love mercy, and walk
humbly with you.

In Jesus' name,

Amen.

VASHTI MURPHY MCKENZIE is bishop of the Thirteenth Episcopal
District of the African Methodist Episcopal Church and was the first
woman to be consecrated bishop in this historic denomination. After
experience as a journalist, she served as a pastor and then bishop in southern Africa. She is author of *Not without a Struggle: Leadership Development for
African-American Women in Ministry* (1996) and several other books.

For Repentance

Creator God of prophetic voices and priestly virtues, whose
almighty presence reminds us that we are the children of

majestic power and eternal light. We are captured by your divine creativity that produces us. We thank you for your Son and our Savior, Jesus Christ, whose steadfast grace and mercy save us from ourselves. We thank you for your eternal kingdom that provides the impetus for our hope in Jesus Christ. We thank you for standing through the ages in faithfulness to our indolence of spirit. May our thanksgiving be met with the everlasting source of abundant grace that sustains us through all of our faults and frailties.

O God of Abraham, Isaac, and Jacob, the grace and mercy you extend is profound amid our fallen and broken world communities. We often lose sight of our need for you and one another. Consequently, while nations are fighting senseless wars, our communities are impoverished and turned upside down. You called us to exude creativity through living in peace, and we construct weapons to alienate other pilgrims on this journey called life. May we be as willing to live for peace as we are to die for power.

Precious Spirit of Ruth, Rebekah, and Lydia, we are living in a land where crack dealers have become community philanthropists as they pay a poor single mother's rent. In turn these same death merchants use the mother's children as "lookouts for the police." While we compete for esthetic beauty by erecting multibillion-dollar skyscrapers, death looms beneath these monuments of our own self-gratification in the form of inner-city violence, "drive-by" shootings, and "car-jackings." O God of Creation, we are charged with the responsibility to be stewards of your earth. However, we flush our waste into your rivers and streams because we take your goodness for granted. We pollute your air and destroy nature's balance in your forests through our overzealous desires to be greedy. Embrace our wayward tendencies to distance ourselves from your will. Precious Lord, we pray that you use these moments when we are spiritually destitute to remind us that there is a reservoir of renewal in which the newness of life never runs dry.

Lord God of the Ages, call your church universal into repentance. Amid the swelling tide of relief needed throughout the world, our silence is deafening to your still small voice, which attempts to speak through us as a vessel of human transformation. We fail to address the dominance, power, control, and structural flaws that lead to racial alienation, gender discrimination, and economic deprivation. Lord, have mercy on us and restore us as your hope for our world. Help us possess a soul of righteousness within us, so that justice may be proclaimed throughout the earth. To this end, may your continued faithfulness heal the wounded and restore the misunderstood. In your mercy, help us to be doers of your word!

THE REV. DR. J. HERBERT NELSON II is pastor of Liberation Community Presbyterian Church (U.S.A.) in Memphis, Tennessee. Nelson, a third-generation Presbyterian pastor, founded the church in 1999 as a ministry that evangelizes the poor to the PC(USA). The African-centered ministry is involved in a myriad of ministries designed to provide a context for individual and communal empowerment. His wife, Gail Porter Nelson, is pastor of the Peace Lutheran Church, also in Memphis.

For the Transformation of Society*

Our Father, who welcomes the prodigal
and who like a mother cares for all,
turn us so that we may hold your name holy above
    worldly powers,

*Rauschenbusch began his own book of prayers with a distinctly social interpretation of the Lord's Prayer. Before God, Rauschenbusch believed, all constitute one community, one family, and Jesus' prayer looks forward to the regeneration and reconstitution of human relations according to the will of God. This prayer is not meant to be an alternative version of the Lord's Prayer, but rather a brief commentary that emphasizes its sometimes neglected social meaning.

that your reign of justice and peace may finally
   come to earth
and that your will may be done here as in heaven.
Give us daily nourishment
that we may be strengthened in your service.
Forgive the wrongs we have done
and help us to forgive those who have wronged us
that enmity and violence may cease
and that all persons and communities may know
   your reconciling grace.
Keep us from those temptations and trials we
   cannot bear,
and deliver us in our struggles with evil.
For the kingdom of righteousness,
the power of reconciliation,
and the glory of all creation and new creation
are yours this day and forever.
Amen.

DOUGLAS F. OTTATI, Craig Family Professor of Reformed Theology and Justice Ministry at Davidson College, taught for many years at Union-PSCE in Richmond, Virginia. A self-described liberal theologian, he is an elder in the Presbyterian Church (U.S.A.) as well as the author of several books and a general editor of the Library of Theological Ethics.

That We May Enlarge Our Hearts

Spirit of the living God,
fall afresh on us,
"we can never be born too many times."*

*e.e. cummings

You who grieve any diminished communion
and the death of any of Earth's beauty;
you who send us the cries for justice of our critics
and the song of the wounded,
cleave the hardened soil of our complacency,
and save us from taming the dreams of the
    prophets.

Keep us from making commitments our lives
    do not confirm,
and standing firm against sins we were never
    tempted to commit.
Enlarge our hearts to all suffering,
and empower us to be worthy renewers of social
    Christianity.
Stir us up, body, mind, and spirit,
and set us on the Way.

Amen.

LARRY RASMUSSEN is professor emeritus at Union Theological
Seminary in New York City. He is author of numerous books in envi-
ronmental and economic ethics. In 1997, he won the Grawemeyer
Award for his book *Earth Community, Earth Ethics* (1996). He coordi-
nates a program in environmental theology at Ghost Ranch, New
Mexico.

That We May Love God
and Our Neighbors

Gracious God, Lord of Creation,
    We are humbled by the intricacy and vastness of your
work. Although we gladly sing your praise, our voices
tremble into silence at the limits of our understanding. For

like Job we have agonizing questions about the suffering we see around us.

Jesus assures us that you love your creation, even us. In astonished gratitude and confidence in your steadfast care, we offer you our fragile love and dare to lift up before you the oppression, suffering, injustices, and torments that afflict your children.

Forgive us that we have failed in the two sacred tasks you have asked of us: to love you above all and to love our neighbors as ourselves. We confess that we inflict much pain, suffering, poverty, disease, and violence in its many forms upon one another in your beautiful world.

In the anguish of our shame we beg you to forgive us and to strengthen us anew rightly to worship you:

by imaginative and wise caring for one another, near and far;

by tending our rare, precious planet, glowing and pulsing with life;

by living with empathy and hope, courage and faithful persistence in active pursuit of your will for us all;

by seeking a generous peace among nations and neighbors, families and strangers; and

by working toward what not only serves our country but what benefits global humanity.

Thank you for hearing our prayer, uttered in our own name and with the encouragement of Jesus.

Amen.

PEGGY LEU SHRIVER has held positions of research, evaluation, and planning in both the former Presbyterian Church, U.S. national offices and the National Council of Churches. She has authored six books, including two of poetry, and has been involved in numerous social justice issues locally and nationally.

To Find the Right Balance

O God, we give you thanks and praise for granting us nimble minds and eager hearts to engage the world around us and, in so doing, to better our lives and those of others. In our best moments, we have used our abilities to bring about the equality between races and sexes that you intended. We have endeavored to care for the most vulnerable among us, old and young, poor and sick. And we have sought to govern with true compassion, sharing our wealth as best we can with your children around the globe.

But we mourn when your name and teachings are wielded as political weapons, to divide, to vanquish, and to silence. We confess that we have enabled this sin by letting others speak in your name. We have too often stayed silent, for fear of being ridiculed or in the belief that your divine realm must not enter into our worldly matters. We have allowed hate to be spoken in your name and have not stood up to rebuke those responsible. We are truly sorry, and we humbly repent.

Help us, we pray, to find the right balance. We seek to pray quietly in our most inner rooms, as you taught us, without parading our faith for personal gain. But we also know that you do not want us to hide our lights under our bushels. Let us never be ashamed to be your children nor let others lay sole claim to your words. And may we be ever humble, remembering at all times that even as we labor in your service, we can never be fully certain of our own judgments. For all have sinned and fallen short of your glory, even those who capture a majority of the votes in the electoral college.

When we enter into the political realm, grant us the wisdom to discern your will, the strength not to confuse it with our own, and the courage to carry it out. Let our light so shine before all that they may see our good works and glorify you in heaven.

AMY SULLIVAN is the nation editor for *Time* magazine, where she directs political coverage and the magazine's polling operation. Her book, *The Party Faithful: How and Why Democrats are Closing the God Gap*, was published in February 2008 by Scribner. Sullivan's work has appeared in publications including the *Los Angeles Times*, *The New Republic*, *Slate*, and *The Washington Post*, and was included in *The Best Political Writing 2006*.

For Those Torn Apart by Violence

O God, we confess that we are a fearful people. Each day we grow more afraid of those who are different rather than becoming more open to embracing that difference as the mysterious and marvelous gift you intend it to be. We assume the worst intentions in those whom we meet, and all too often we act in ways that fan further the flames of mistrust, causing the culture of fear to grow greater each day.

As our fear grows, O God, we find ourselves incapable of the simple act of placing our trust in you. You call us to love our enemies and all those whose intentions — real or perceived — might be to harm us, yet we respond with overwhelming military might intended to "shock and awe" our enemies with our power. We justify our actions with blind nationalism and a patriotism that gives lie to our profession that we trust in you alone.

We weep with you, O God, for countless families that have been torn apart by violence and war in places we have sent our military in a thinly disguised attempt to extend our economic hegemony around the world. We confess our complicity in the vicious spiral of violence that grows steeper with each passing day. We search for cheap labor and natural resources to quench our insatiable thirst to consume. We take what we want at the point of a gun or a missile. We misread the resistance to our tyranny by sisters and brothers around the world as an irrational hate that must be met by force. We turn to simple, foolish answers of violence as we feel more and more afraid. We are seduced by the ways in which we ourselves profit from our involvement in the vast military-industrial complex that drives us deeper and deeper into war.

We confess, O God, that we are numbed by our media's unrelenting reports of irrational acts of terror. Even as we are repulsed, something inside us continues to be drawn inexplicably toward the commodification of suffering. As a result, we fail to recognize the ways in which our own participation in the violence of war is antithetical to all that is at the heart of your liberating message of hope.

O God, we long for the day when those who make plans for war learn instead that there is great profit in peace. We dream of the day when we ourselves will learn to seek our own security in an attitude of humility rather than hostility. We commit to you, O God, that we will begin by confronting the reality of our own privilege in the world, and by confessing the ways in which we refuse to unlearn racism that has been so deeply ingrained in us. We will strive to let power fall away; to let love replace fear; to build relationships marked by trust, respect, and fairness with sisters and brothers in our own communities and around the world.

Finally, O God, we give thanks for acts of courage by your people that point the way to a new day. We are grateful for the discomfort we feel that signals an awakening of the passion for peace only you can ignite in our souls. We are in awe of the glimpses you offer of the beloved community that is within our grasp: Christian peacemakers who become a nonviolent presence in communities marked by long-standing resentments, grave injustice, and the seeds of hate; moments of reconciliation between peoples long separated by fear; small expressions of community in which your people have defied boundaries, torn down borders, and ignored the barriers that divide us.

We are yours, O God. From this day forward we give ourselves to you, knowing that the cost may be great but that the alternative is capitulation to the forces of death.

Stand with us, we pray, O God. Give us courage. Do not allow us to fail. We are yours.

RICK UFFORD-CHASE, a Presbyterian layperson, was the youngest Moderator of the General Assembly elected in the Presbyterian Church (U.S.A.) in decades. From leading Borderlinks, an education and mission program on the United States/Mexico border, he has now become director of the Presbyterian Peace Fellowship and is heavily involved in the Christian peace witness for Iraq.

<hr />

That I May Be Transfigured

I am the one, O Lord.

I'm the one concerning whom a number of prayers herein are prayed—

The one against whose behaviors the saints make supplication:

"Stretch forth your hand; by signs and wonders, diminish the oppressor's oppressions."

Wherefore I can in my prayer do no better than confess my sins and beg your gracious, transfiguring grace.

For, though I have lived among (have *loved*) the impoverished, yet I (in spite of the gift of such knowing) have chosen to house myself, to dress and transport myself, to entertain myself at home and abroad, in a manner which the poor—yes, even the *working* poor—can do no more than dream about.

For I have spent as if I myself were the object of all my spending and the owner of all my goods. I have justified the wretched disparity by believing in the rightness and the value of my work, and hence in my deserving.

For though my work is meant to serve, I am no servant. I have my reward. I take private shots of pleasure in each of my well-doings; ministry elevates my spirit above others; pride permits me to sleep at peace with myself, under the shining sheets of my goodness in the world—and so I am justified in living higher than those my good work serves.

Transfigure me, my Christ!

For I by a mindless participation have approved of those systems which benefit powerful corporations, both national and global. I am their blood. Daily I circulate through the pipes of power *(give-a-little, get-a-little)*, granting advantages for them and for me, granting growth to a machinery whose only purpose is to exist and to *grow*, feeding upon the bones of the weak, the poor, workers without alternatives, families with two jobs and endless debt.

For I buy foods whose prices rise according to the increasing distances they must travel to get to my store: my bread is baked of tire rubber, truck maintenance, road maintenance, and diesel fuel; its ingredients shipped from places distant to bakeries in other distant places, to be sold. . . . I drive a personal vehicle to the neglect of public transportation, causing busses and trains to raise prices or else to cut their routes, in either case leaving the poor whipsawed, standing in the cold.

Forgive me, Jesus. Make me yours, in deed as well as in my conceiving.

For I by a savvy rhetoric condemn the government's various oppressions, crushing persons and peoples. I denounce its warring postures, its unreasonable secrecies, its shreddings of individual rights, its intrusions upon democratic acts by power and by manipulations. I am not blind. I recognize the iniquities of the powers surrounding me.

But I do not *do*. I'd rather not inconvenience myself by a serious sacrificial action, or jeopardize my reputation (my own small power to do good things!) by rising against the lifestyles of the masses.

For I have chosen my ease above your commandments—

For I know, I *know* how one proclaims the advent of the kingdom of heaven: by becoming a wave in that ocean's advent: *Cure the sick. Raise the dead. Cleanse the lepers. Cast out demons. You (I) received without paying; so give without receiving pay. Take no gold or silver or copper in your pockets, not bag for your journey, neither two tunics nor sandals nor a staff*—

Christ, transfigure me!

For the evidence of forgiveness is change in the individual forgiven. And the evidence is the healing of those whom the sinner has wounded.

Forgive me, cause me joyfully to benefit your children:

—elevating the weak, humanizing the heartless,
—being the kingdom of heaven in order to proclaim it.

Amen.

WALTER WANGERIN JR. joined Valparaiso University's faculty in 1991 as the Emil and Elfriede Jochum University Professor. Wangerin first came into national prominence as the author of *The Book of the Dun Cow* (1978), which won the National Book Award. He is widely known as a speaker, storyteller, and the author of more than thirty books, ranging from fiction to children's stories to practical theology and devotionals, working out of the Lutheran tradition.

9

POEMS, SONG, AND LITANIES

Tingling Thoughts

It is but You,
You, who pulled the mountains from the ground,
You, to whom every creature is bound,
You, who pressed the lands and forged oceans,
You, who filled the minds with unseen notions,
You, who has never forgotten the ants nor the
    huge camels,
You, who created all life from insects to mammals,
You, who already knows what I'm about to write,
You, who stands by me in the ease and the plight,
I ask you to shed Your radiant light
on me and on us, to open our thoughts,
to end our fight.

Unheard feelings undulated through the air,
and sent out signals, like a night where thunders
    bestow glare.
But that thunder like whisper murmured in my ears;
that power like shower rained out my fears.

But before that circle that was not the case,
You know my mind was shut, and my eyes the truth
would erase.
Yet my door was knocked on like tick-tock open
your gate.
Tick-Tock slow down, your now is here;
openness awaits.
Tick-Tock your hands are lonely, so lend them to me.
Tick-Tock your lands but only to be shared with thee.
Tick-Tock your chains be broken when I say,
Knock-Knock your words have spoken, "Let's pray!"

In the dimness I limbed and saw the knob with
virgin eyes,
but the knob would never turn, I thought, and I could
never rise.
True, the keyhole was always there, but I was afraid
to stare
until the day my heart, my life, and me became
aware
that in this we are not alone, and from here we
could begin.
Suddenly, the door from the other side was
pushed open.
We gave birth to peace at a pinky sunset.
The ears were listening, and the eyes were wet.
O God, I thank you for every moment you plan
for me,
for every moment I was there, the late hours
and the wee.
After all, it is but You who split the worlds
into the stars.
And it is but You who creates peace from scars.
From You we start, and to You we end,
and to You . . . our praise we send.

ABDULLAH A. YAHYA is a Muslim born in Iraq who now lives in Denver. He was seventeen years old when he began participating in the Face to Face/Faith to Faith program sponsored by Auburn Seminary. Face to Face/Faith to Faith enables participants to see how their own religion calls them to engage in public and world issues; nurtures an understanding of other religions, cultures, and people; and increases their ability to collaborate along lines of religion, culture, class, and ethnicity to make a better world.

A Hymn for the Bees

With the Spirit, John came to the Jordan,
baptizing for repentance and forgiveness
    of sins;
prophesying and eating honey,
tasting of the kingdom of God.

And the bees . . .
they rejoiced with the cherubim
and the seraphim.
Their hives hummed with a hymn
    to heaven.

But now there is silence.
The music has stopped.
The hives are empty.
The bees have gone.
No one knows why
    or where.

Did we drive them from
their dormant dwellings
with demons we invited?

The Lord has said to us
"I have prepared a place for you
with fruit-laden trees
and springs flowing
with milk and honey" (based on 2 Esd. 2:19).

Yet we are ripping from
    Farmland and forest
The trees on whose blossoms
The bees thrive —
The tulip and willow,
Black cherry and locust;

And pouring poison
On the clover and dandelion,
Banishing the bees
    From our lives.

Factories cannot manufacture honeycomb.
The kingdom will not rise from
    Suburban subdivisions.
Manicured lawns mock green pastures.
Their sterility scorns the fertile womb
In which Paradise has been restored.

The Spirit has taken flight with the bees.
Pray for the bees!

VIGEN GUROIAN is an Armenian Orthodox theologian. He lives in
Culpeper, Virginia, with his wife, June, where he mostly tends to his
large perennial beds and vegetable garden and keeps bees. He is the
author of numerous books and articles, including *Inheriting Paradise:
Meditations on Gardening*, *The Fragrance of God*, and *Tending the Heart of
Virtue: How Classic Stories Awaken a Child's Moral Imagination*.

To Trust in God the Giver of Justice*

One: Praise the Lord! Praise the Lord, O my
soul!

All: I will praise the Lord as long as I live. I will
sing praises to God all my life long!

One: Do not put your trust in princes or in mortals
in whom there is no help; when their breath
departs they return to the earth and their plans
perish.

All: We will trust in God who is our Creator and
who is the source of our help!

One: Happy are those whose help is the God of
Jacob, whose hope is in the Lord who made
heaven and earth, who keeps faith forever.

All: We will trust in God who is the source of our
faith and who calls us to live into hope!

One: It is God who executes justice for the
oppressed, who gives food to the hungry and
who sets the prisoners free.

All: We will trust in God the giver of justice who
calls us to do justice!

One: It is the Lord who opens the eyes of the blind,
who lifts up those who are bowed down and
heavy burdened.

All: We will trust the Lord who heals and who calls
us to be healers!

One: It is the Lord who watches over the stranger in
the land, who upholds the orphan, the widow,
and the outcast.

*An Affirmation of Faith based on Psalm 146

All: We will trust the Lord of compassion who calls us to empower the powerless and show loving-kindness to outcasts!

One: The Lord will reign forever; the justice of God shall be for all people and unto all generations.

All: Praise the Lord, the giver of justice, the source of our faith, the sustainer of our hope, the Spirit of loving-kindness. Thanks be to God! Amen!

THE REV. DR. NILE HARPER is a Presbyterian minister and director of Urban Church Research in Minneapolis. He was professor of church and society at New York Theological Seminary and professor of sociology of religion in the Schools of Theology in Dubuque (Presbyterian, Lutheran, Catholic), and is author of *Urban Churches, Vital Signs* and other books.

A Prophetic Trailblazer's Psalm

O Divine Spirit,
who anointed with zeal the prophet of Galilee,
come singe my heart so I may recall
that by my baptism into Christ
you also ordained me to prophethood.

Forgive my self-pardoning for all failings
to live out that vocation by limiting prophets
to ancient days and faraway biblical lands.

Arouse me to my destiny and inspire me
to replace the biblical *prophet* with *trailblazer*.

Remind me that Jesus was your fearless trailblazer,
who cut pathways out of dead, ritualized religion
and inflexible, restricting social conventions.

As his trailblazer disciple
emblazon me to go places where others fear to go,
to cross closed social barriers and closed minds,
to open new inroads into the ruthless prison domains
of crippling poverty and racial and sexual
    discrimination,
and to make a springtime path through the wastelands
of injustices in labor, health care, and education.

Divine Giver of Destinies,
inspire me to live out my destiny courageously
by blazing trails beyond the borders
of religion and societal conventions.

Spur my soul to strike out, even alone if necessary,
to boldly mark out the path to that
promised land of God's justice and peace.

EDWARD HAYS is a Catholic priest who has directed a contempla-
tive center in Kansas while writing a score of books, including several
prayer books. An artist, storyteller, and liturgical theologian, his books
include playful invitations to prayer and other ways of seeing God's
world.

Real Presence

Yes, a frilly pink tutu
was, more or less — more less
than more — all he wore,
that and a tall pair of teetering
stiletto heels and parasol — from tip
to toe in matching lurid pink,
strutting his jet-glow black and

body-built stuff from side to side
in flagrant full gay pride
parading down Fifth Avenue.

From giant urns outside our church
we plied the passers-by with plastic
cups "o'kindness yet" on a hot June
afternoon — "in Jesus' Name."
Fully clothed, and more,
dark clergy suit, black shirt and
stiff white collar, I stood my ground,
clutching a tray of cooling draughts
to represent a welcome and a blessing —
at the least — as child of God.

Beaming, he tripped across bestowing
smiles, spectacular, on all and sundry,
chiefly me. Daintily he took the cup
I offered, leaned perilous close —
those tipping heels! — and kissed me on one
startled cheek, his bristles coarse, lips —
generous smile notwithstanding — brushing
deep, appalled revulsion through my gut,
despite all my head was murmuring of
tolerance and Christian love.

"O Reverend," laughed the lady
from the sewing circle,
"you should see the juicy kiss
mark on your cheek." And as we both
dissolved in honest, healing mirth,
first head, then heart took over
from my gut and raised a prayer
of thanks for grace's all-too-often
way of shoving me, still screaming,
toward birth.

J. BARRIE SHEPHERD, a Presbyterian pastor and well-published poet, grew up in Scotland, served in the Royal Air Force, and was minister to well-known pastorates in Swarthmore, Pennsylvania, and New York City. His books include meditations on Scripture and prayer diaries; his poetry shows a constant delight in the play of words.

For a Service of Ordination

Leader: Holy One our God, God of all generations, we affirm your goodness that has not left us helpless but provides us with instruction through your Holy Word. We give you thanks for your grace that calls your servants ever anew to work in the vineyard of your creation.

All: May they abide with strength and courage and patience for the tasks you provide for hand and mind.

Leader: You have sent us your prophets and set them afire with visions of life as you intend it.

All: May our hearts and will be open to their words of truth and encouragement, to their story of hope, their holy restlessness.

Leader: We commend to you, most holy and marvelous Creator, your servants as they prepare to serve you in a special function, that they may continue what you have begun in them, that they may speak words of truth and inspire us with visions of life as you intend it.

All: May they draw us into the future toward the new world you are creating in us, among us, and through us by the power of your Spirit.

Leader: You give us visions of a new world, O God, yet we find it easy to abide in the old. You promise your presence among us, yet we seek our own way out of life's wilderness.

All: O God, grant us new life in you!

Leader: We have heard that you created the world beautiful and good and that it is your desire for there to be no distinctions of hierarchy and no dominations among us; yet we abide in the domination of one sex over another, of one race over another, of one religion over another.

All: To you, O God, we turn for guidance; turn to us and help us.

Leader: O God, grant us new life, so that the saying "neither Jew nor Greek, neither slave nor free, no male and female" may become real among us. Take from us the desire to possess the exclusive path to your loving heart, the wish to be the only ones that may live inside the house of your loving-kindness.

All: To you, O God, we turn for understanding; turn to us and help us.

Leader: Teach us to glory in the complexity of your creation, to celebrate your holiness in the difference that meets us in the other race, the other sex, the other class, the other faith. Wipe away our fear of the unknown, our obsession with the known. Make us a pilgrim people in Jesus' name.

All: To you, O God, we turn for meaning; turn to us and help us.

Leader: God, our redeemer and friend, you have given us the power of imagination, through which the future grasps our lives today. Teach us discernment, wise hearts to recog-

nize you in the face of the other, the face of
the stranger.

All: O God, grant us new life in you!

Leader: God of our future, we trust in the great promises of liberation and healing you provided for
all humanity through your people Israel and
your child Jesus, whom we confess as Christ.
We know that our true home is with you and
that for this home we yearn. We have heard
that in your house justice and love flourish to
bring peace and health to all who live in it.
Give us courage and patience and love to be
ministers of this house where the bruised reed
is not broken and the flickering candle is not
snuffed out. We know that with you brokenness is welcomed and healed. Give us the
grace to be so welcoming and healing to all
who suffer in our communities from the
scourges of our time. Make of us a bulwark
against the hatreds that consume us, of class
or sex or race, and against the lust for power
and domination make us a sure defense.

All: Today is the acceptable time, now is the
dawning of hope. Make us lovers and healers and doers of justice. Not tomorrow, not
some day, but now.

Amen.

JOHANNA W. H. VAN WIJK-BOS is an ordained Presbyterian minister and is the Dora Pierce Professor of Bible and Professor of Old Tes-
tament at Louisville Presbyterian Theological Seminary in Louisville,
Kentucky. She teaches courses in Hebrew language, exegesis of
the Bible, biblical theology, and liberationist and feminist theology and
is actively involved in the Women's Center at the seminary. Besides
many reviews and articles she has written eight books, the latest of
which, *Making Wise the Simple — The Torah in Christian Faith and Practice*,
appeared in 2005.

A Pilgrim's Hymn

G D/F# G
I will set my feet upon the road.
   C   D   G
I will follow wherever you lead.
(repeat)
  G   C   G
I know not where the road will end.
  G   C   D
I know not what is up around the bend,
  G D/F# G
but I will set my feet upon the road.
    C   D   G
I will follow wherever you lead.

Was that you I met along the road?
Was that you walking with me?
(repeat)
I was fine all on my own,
but you taught me things I never could have known.
Was that you I met along the road?
Was that you walking with me?

There are those who sit along the road.
As I walk, they call out to me.
(repeat)
They are blind, and they are lame.
Will I pass them; will I cause them pain?
There are those who sit along the road.
As I walk, they call out to me.

I reach out and take them by the hand.
I ask them to walk with me.

(repeat)
They tell me of the life they've known,
all the heartaches, all the ways they've grown.
I reach out and take them by the hand.
I ask them to walk with me.

It grows late, and I am going tired.
They ask me to rest with them.
(repeat)
And as we talk, my strength renews,
and I can see their beauty; I can see their truth.
It grows late, and I am going tired.
They ask me to rest with them.

I drift off in the stillness of the night,
but something calls me back.
(repeat)
The many around me have become one,
and they are shining brightly like the sun.
I drift off in the stillness of the night,
but something calls me back.

LANDON WHITSITT is pastor at the First Presbyterian Church in
Liberty, Missouri. He has been the music leader for several local congregations, national conferences, and regional retreats, and has pro-
duced an album of worship titled *Ordo* (which features "A Pilgrim's
Hymn"). Previously, he cowrote and edited a book of daily prayer for
young adults titled *Connect: A New Guide for Daily Prayer*. His music and
writing can been found online at http://www.landonville.com, where
one can download a free mp3 of "A Pilgrim's Hymn."